Victims of Crime
and Punishment

ALSO BY SHIRLEY DICKS

From Vietnam to Hell: Interviews with
Victims of Post-Traumatic Stress Disorder
(McFarland, 1990; paperback 2012)

Death Row: Interviews with Inmates,
Their Families and Opponents of Capital Punishment
(McFarland, 1990; paperback 2012)

Victims of Crime and Punishment

Interviews with Victims, Convicts, Their Families, and Support Groups

Shirley Dicks

McFarland & Company, Inc., Publishers

Jefferson, North Carolina, and London

The present work is a reprint of the softcover edition of Victims of Crime and Punishment: Interviews with Victims, Convicts, Their Families, and Support Groups, *first published in 1991 by McFarland.*

Library of Congress Cataloguing-in-Publication Data

Dicks, Shirley, 1940–
    Victims of crime and punishment : interviews with victims, convicts, their families, and support groups / by Shirley Dicks.
        p.   cm.
    Includes index.

    ISBN 978-0-7864-6945-1
    softcover : acid free paper ∞

    1. Victims of crimes — United States — Interviews.
    2. Prisoners — United States — Interviews.   I. Title.
    HV6250.3.U5D53 2012
    362.88'0973 — dc20   91-52753

British Library cataloguing data are available

Front cover design by David K. Landis (Shake It Loose Graphics)

Manufactured in the United States of America

McFarland & Company, Inc., Publishers
    Box 611, Jefferson, North Carolina 28640
        www.mcfarlandpub.com

*This book is dedicated
to my youngest son, Trevor Richard Dicks.
He was the victim of a violent mugging
in Knoxville, Tennessee, in 1990.*

Contents

I. Victims of Crime

Personal Accounts

Support and Survival

II. Victims of Punishment

Personal Accounts

Support and Voices for Reform

Part I: Victims of Crime

Personal Accounts

Debbie C. Darbois-Lowe

Daughter of Murder Victim

"My father's entire life was filled with a love of automobiles. My grandmother has told me stories of how he would play in my grandparents' car at a very young age and drive it around their property in West Virginia for hours. He married my mother when he was 19 and was working as a mechanic even before that. I am the oldest of five children, and I remember my father as a mechanic. He was partners with a friend who raced stock cars at the car races in Canton, Ohio. I remember pictures of me sitting on his race car wearing a helmet with my mother standing alongside, pregnant with my sister. That is why it is so ironic that he would die as a result of this love of automobiles, in an indirect manner.

"October 6, 1988, began just as any other day; but shortly after I arrived at work at 8:30 that Thursday morning, I began to have a shaky, uneasy feeling that I just could not explain. It was like you knew something out of the ordinary was going to happen.

"About 9:45 that morning I received a telephone call from my father's wife of five months, and she informed me that my brother had been in an automobile accident and Bayfront Medical Center was requesting a family member at the hospital immediately. After 31 years of marriage, my parents were divorced, as sometimes happens these days. My mother is still living, and all of us children still remain very close to her. When I received the call, I wondered where my father was, since he and my brother had a business together buying, repairing, detailing, and selling cars. This seemed very strange to me, because I knew they started their work day early, as my father had for so many years. How could they be separated so early in the day, and why wasn't my father the one they contacted as the much-needed family member?

"I immediately began to shake and knew I was acting irrational; but I was able to drive my car from Seminole to downtown St. Petersburg, stopping to get gas on the way, at a speed of 80 miles per hour in a 35-mile zone, without a ticket.

"As I entered the emergency area of the hospital, I was met by an ambulance driver who offered his help. I'm sure he could see how upset I was,

3

and I told him why I was there. He said he was going to get the chaplain, and it was then I knew something was terribly wrong. All the way to the hospital I had heard over the radio of a shooting at a Pinellas Park business, where a gunman was holding a hostage and someone had been shot. They mentioned a .357 gun. Now I found that this was my father's business they were talking about. The chaplain was reluctant to give me too much information and I later learned he was told not to by the police department.

"The chaplain knew then that my father was dead, but he could not tell me. He said my brother had been shot, and it hadn't been an automobile accident like I'd been told. He was in surgery right then after being brought in by helicopter, but he was still alive. The chaplain did tell me that someone was dead, but he didn't elaborate. He said that I should get my family together at the hospital, but he wouldn't tell me anything about my father.

"I tried calling my father on his beeper but he wouldn't answer. Where in God's name was he? I couldn't believe this was happening and I felt as if I were in a dream. This is something you read about, something that does not happen to you.

"Since I was the first one to arrive at the hospital, I immediately got on the phone to call other family members to get them to the hospital. Maybe one of them would know where my father was. I couldn't readily reach anyone by telephone, but kept trying. My sister found out of the shooting by her girlfriend who had heard it on the news and she was on the way to the hospital. Another sister had heard by our grandmother who also heard it on the news. My grandmother received a call from a reporter asking how she felt now that her son was dead. She had not been informed by a family member or anyone in a compassionate manner; she was harassed by the news media.

"I made the mistake of calling my mother at work and told her that my brother had been shot. She fainted, and someone at the shop had to bring her to the hospital. If I had it to do over, I would have told her the same story they told me, that he had been in an automobile accident. Still not one told us of my father's whereabouts.

"The comfort of my family was not enough during those hours of waiting. I telephoned my boyfriend and he immediately came to the hospital to be with me. He is now my husband and I don't know what I would have done without him, not just during those moments, but through all the pain I have gone through since then. I know he will always be there for me to get through my bad dreams and pain.

"For hours we were held in a small waiting room at the hospital without the slightest inclination of what had happened, of my brother's condition, or where my father was. While we waited, others were watching television and learning of the shooting, seeing pictures, and they knew my father was dead. We were told not to leave the room, for what reason we still do not exactly know, but can only guess. My father had pled for help from the police department but never received any. It took days after the murder for the Pinellas Park Police Department to bring forth a recorded telephone conversation my father had with an officer asking for help. They did not release the recorded conversation until minutes before a news cast, because they knew they were guilty of wrongdoing and knew they would be found out.

"Finally, two officers came to the hospital waiting room and tried to explain what had happened. (Now I remembered that two weeks earlier my teenage son and my brother, who also worked at the business, came home and expressed dismay that Robert Bickar had on several occasions threatened to kill my father and my brother.) They both seemed disturbed and worried and explained that my father had telephoned the Pinellas Park Police Department searching for some kind of help but was told, 'there is nothing we can do. If someone verbally threatens your life, nothing can be done unless and until they carry out that threat.'

"My father had told the police then that 'chances are, after it happens, I'll be bleeding so bad, I won't be able to report it.' That is exactly what happened.

"We were informed that Robert 'Red' Bickar, a longtime 'friend' of my father who had followed him to Florida from Ohio and who had been a financial partner with him, had come to my father's business carrying two loaded weapons and ammunition. He swore my father owed him money, when in essence he would get his money after some cars were sold. He shot my brother in the leg, with my father immediately charging him, and thereupon he was shot in the chest.

"My brother, with his injured leg, proceeded to run around the huge commercial business complex, searching for help and running for his life, with Bickar chasing him. He ran into a glass glazing business asking for help, and was told to get out because they didn't want to get shot as well. As my brother left the business, he was confronted by Bickar, who shot him through the windows of a van parked in front of the business. He was shot in the face and arm.

"Bickar then proceeded to return to my father's business and finished off my father by shooting him in the head. Bickar then took flares which he had also brought with him, lit them, and threw them into several automobiles located in the building, catching the entire place on fire. He barricaded himself inside while my father lay bleeding and dying in the entrance to the building. By this time SWAT team members had arrived, and my father was pulled from the entrance to the outside. Members of the police department have indicated that they heard some gunfire.

"It was learned that the gunfire was that of Bickar, who had taken his own life. The police waited for the sprinkler system to somewhat put out the fire, and for the smoke to cease, and upon entering found Bickar dead on the ground.

"My brother was taken by helicopter soon after. They had waited to bring it in because of the gunfire. My brother says he remembers his ride in the helicopter and how wonderful the attendants were. He kept telling them to make sure they told his wife how much he loved her because he thought he was going to die. He also remembers how he was treated by the people at the glass glazing business, and says this still hurts him and always will.

"He had heard my father say 'Oh, my God' when he was initially shot and before my brother began to run. Knowing this has helped us all to know that he made his peace with God before he died.

"The next several weeks were a constant vigil at our brother's side. I will never forget the first time I walked into the intensive care unit and saw my brother. His face and neck were swollen, his arms and legs were hurt, and he had a very sad, distant look on his face. He kept asking about Dad, but we didn't dare tell him that he was dead. I think he knew that we were lying to him, and we finally had to tell him the truth. Tears flowed down his face, but he couldn't move because of the injuries.

"Many of us, especially my grandmother, began to receive death threats. Whether they were from the murderer's brother or just a prankster, no one will ever know. The fear was there, no matter who was making the calls, and the police still would not protect and guard my brother. The murderer had sworn he would get my brother first so my dad could watch, and then get my father. If he didn't do the job, he would make sure his brother would.

"What could we do? For the next few weeks at least, we made certain there was a guard at the hospital with my brother, all at the family's expense of course. At least it made him feel a little bit safer. I felt such anger at the Pinellas Park Police, as they were definitely guilty of wrongdoing. I had always thought the police were there to protect us.

"When we went in the shop to change locks, we found a gas mask and a nine millimeter handgun lying on the bumper of one of the cars. These belonged to the police. We found a bullet lying on the work bench, with a blue plastic tip filled with pellets. We have talked to the police and they deny any wrongdoing.

"The Chief of Police even stood behind the rookie cop that took my father's phone call asking for help. If only the officer had called Red Bickar like he promised my father he would do, just maybe it would have scared him off and my father would be alive today.

"One week after the shooting, police released the tape recorded telephone conversation in which Jim Marlor told Officer Mark Brodowski that Bickar had threatened to blow up his business and kill him.

"Following the shooting, Pinellas Park police said they had no record of a call. They said that Officer Brodowski didn't remember talking to anyone by that name. Considering the voluminous print and broadcast media coverage of the shootout, it is difficult to believe that Brodowski would fail to recognize the names given in the telephone call. If he didn't remember the names, then maybe the police department should provide better training for officers who handle citizen complaints.

"Officer Brodowski said that if someone says he's gonna blow up your business or he's gonna kill you, there's nothing illegal about doing that . . . until he makes some effort toward carrying it out. At this time Marlor replied, 'Yeah, chances are, after it happens, I'll be bleeding so bad I won't be able to report it. I'm trying to stop trouble before it happens.'

"Thank God my brother remains such a healthy young man. After several weeks, he could communicate with us by writing what he wanted to say, and then he could cap off his tracheotomy and make sounds. We feared he would never be able to talk again because one of the bullets had ricocheted off his jaw, shattering it, and hit his tongue. His tendon in his arm was damaged and he had no movement, so we feared he would never be able to use it again.

"All through this constant vigil, my brother's wife slept in his hospital room and was by his side constantly. She is a gymnastics instructor, as well as a karate expert, and competed very earnestly, as she wanted to be the first in the world one day. During this time she fell behind, but with God's will and determination, she is now a silver medalist.

"The planning of Dad's memorial was one of the worst pains we had to endure. Since he wanted to be cremated, we followed his wishes. We picked out a beautiful oak urn, and had a plaque engraved and placed on the front which read 'Dearly Loved by His Family.' The service was beautiful, and the chapel was filled to the brim, with people flowing out the doors. Because of the death threats, we had two plainclothed police officers on the premises; and as I was not acting rational, I had emptied my purse and carried a loaded .357 in my purse and placed myself at the front of the chapel. Seeing our grandmother's pain as she endured the memorial service was almost unbearable. She had lost our grandfather to whom she would have been married 62 years had he lived, and now she had lost a son.

"Throughout the next several months, I began to drink excessively and although I didn't really get drunk, I was drinking constantly. I couldn't go back to work and didn't trust anyone. When I finally did go back to work, I couldn't perform properly and lost my job. In the next year, I had a total of six jobs. It was then I began counseling with the Homicide Survivors Group for a 12-week period and began somewhat of a healing process. During my counseling period I drove my car with a bumper sticker which read, "Someone I Love Was Murdered."

"For Thanksgiving the family came to my home for dinner. My brother was out of the hospital, with his jaw wired shut, but for a short time they removed the wires so he could stuff himself with dinner turkey. This was the most dramatic family dinner any of us have ever experienced, but the love that surrounded us will never be forgotten. The holidays were terrible and all any of us could think of was Dad.

"The first part of January 1989, all five of us children rented a van, and with my brother's jaw still wired shut, traveled from Florida to West Virginia with my father's ashes, to have a service performed with the rest of his family present at the home place in Oak Hill, West Virginia. (The home place is a very old home in Oak Hill where my uncle Charlie Miller's family lived for years. My uncle Charlie is married to my father's sister, Jean, and both are wonderful people. When my uncle's mother died, the remaining children of the family decided to keep the property for family gatherings and the like.)

"The trip made us all close, but the pain was almost unbearable for all of us. Seeing our family members, and mostly our grandmother, since she had moved from Florida right after the murder, was wonderful. She is dead now, and I miss her very much. All my life she had been a good friend to me, and I will never forget her.

"The anger which has been felt by all of us was, and remains, almost unbearable. No one deserves to die in such a brutal way, and it could have been prevented if the system worked differently, if the system worked for the people. In fact, so many people would still be alive today, from young children brutalized by either their parents or some other deranged individual, to the old woman who is robbed and raped by the drug addict needing money badly. We are all victims; and we must work together to change the system and maybe someday there will not be so many victims.

"For such a long time I wanted to strike out at anyone I could. But what good would it do? I also get angry when I hear someone complain about their aches and pains; I feel they just do not know what life is about. I felt cheated because the murderer killed himself, and would not be punished, when in essence he was punished before he murdered my father. His family are victims also, and giving pain to another will not stop our pain. I try to stay as close to God and my religion as is humanly possible, and hope that my pain will become lesser as time goes on.

"I work in a law office and constantly see what people do to one another. The whole concept of life is totally out of control. What happened to the idea of helping our neighbor, instead of suing them? Whatever happened to family life? Divorce is so rampant, and the children of the future end up paying for it. These are our criminals of the future. How can we expect children to learn to be kind and good to others when they hear the bitter words and hate that is exchanged each day?

"We need a better prison system and we need a better judicial system. I have written letter after letter in an effort to make changes; but what good is just one person's efforts? Our legislators must begin to work for the people and remember what they are here for. Let's give everyone a fair trial, a fair chance at life. Let's rehabilitate our criminals, and hopefully they will realize whatever it might be that caused them to act out a crime is never a good enough reason to hurt another person. Let's punish properly, wherein punishment causes the act to not be carried out again, and let's teach our children to love and not hate. I feel sorry for Red Bickar, because evidently he did not have the love of a wonderful family as I have."

Trevor Dicks

Mugging Victim

"My wife and I had decided to move to Tennessee as I had a job painting. I was going to live temporarily with my mother and father, who lived in a small trailer along with my younger sister. Until I could get settled in an apartment my wife was going to stay with her mother for a few weeks before joining me. She was expecting our first child in September and wanted to be with her family. I was taking a carload of our dishes and things over to my mother's. I planned to come back the following weekend for more.

"Making the trip in one day was critical because I was to start my new job the next morning. When I got to Knoxville, my car started cutting out on me, so I pulled off the interstate and stopped at a garage to find out what was wrong. They didn't know, so I started fooling with it to see if I could figure out what was wrong. One place told me that it sounded like the alternator, but I didn't have quite enough money to get one put on.

"It was getting late and I decided to find a motel. I didn't really want to spend our little bit of money that way. I hitched a ride with another boy who was in town for a concert. As we were heading down the street, we came to a red light. Suddenly, two big black guys holding a gun jumped in front of the car. The gun was pointed at our heads. I told the boy to step on it and take our chances, but he stopped the engine.

"They screamed at us to get out of the car, and with that gun pointed at us, we had no other choice. The one with the gun ordered us to hand over our wallets. Then he tried to tear my wedding ring off my finger, but it wouldn't come off. I was afraid that it wasn't going to come off and didn't like the look on his face. I pulled hard and finally it came off. I didn't want him to cut it off.

"Once they had all our money, they said they wanted more. When we said we didn't have anything else, they told us to take off our clothes, and when I hesitated, he asked me didn't I know that he was holding a nine-millimeter gun in his hand, and that it would blow my head clean off. I tried to talk nice to him, but he had hatred burning in his eyes. Quickly I started peeling off my clothes, hoping they would let us go, but I didn't really think they would. I felt helpless; we couldn't fight back, could do nothing but whatever they told us to do.

"Once we were naked, they shouted at us with an evil laugh. I saw Mike get knocked to the ground—he went down fast, and the boy was kicking him. The one with the gun struck me in the face. I stepped back, determined not to go down. I knew if I did, they would finish us off. Over and over I felt the blows on my face. The pain was unbearable. He was getting madder and madder at me because I wouldn't fall. I watched as the gun went up over his head and came down on my forehead.

"Still I wouldn't go down because I knew they would kill us right then and there. I wanted to fight back, but we were helpless without a gun. I was waiting for the bullet to end my life and fear was running through me. The hate that came from those boys was awful to see. We had done nothing to them, but we were both white boys and that made us the enemy. I saw Mike get up moaning and holding his chest. The boy with the gun looked back to talk to his buddy and I knew they were finished playing with us. It was now or never and I gave Mike a nod. We took off running for our very lives.

"Mike went in one direction and I kept on going straight. I heard the gunshots and was waiting for one of them to hit me. It seemed like I had run forever, up over the interstate where I tried to flag down a trucker. They kept on going. No one would stop. Back to the other side I kept on running, my insides on fire, with pain wracking my whole body. I couldn't go much farther and I prayed that those monsters were gone.

"I saw a laundrymat up ahead and ran in. I collapsed on the floor and a police officer came running in behind me with a blanket. He covered me up and said he had called an ambulance. My whole body was full of pain, and blood was all over. My chest was hurting bad and I thought he had punctured my lung. Once the ambulance arrived, I asked the paramedic if I was dying. He didn't seem to care one way or another and soon I was in the emergency room.

"I begged them to give me something for the pain, but with the blows to the head, they couldn't give me anything. After taking X-rays, they found out that I had three bones broken in my jaw. But with head injuries, they couldn't even set it. The pain was engulfing me and I wanted to strike out at something. I wanted to scream, but I was 22 years old and couldn't do that. I knew my mother would be worried as she had expected me the night before. I called her and she said she'd be there as soon as she could make it. It was a three-hour trip, and I didn't even know what hospital I was in. She said never mind, she would find out when she got there, and I hung up. I felt better knowing my mother was on the way.

"Mom called my wife and she got there in just a few hours. They lived an hour and a half away and made it just before my mother did. I knew I looked awful but the pain was terrible. Finally they were giving me some pain medicine, but nothing penetrated. I felt anger and rage at those boys. I wanted to find them and do to them what they had done to us. I found out that Mike had broken ribs and was on the floor above me. They had stolen his car and the next day the police found it burned.

"The second day I was wheeled into the surgeon's office. He would do the surgery there. He gave me some medicine to almost knock me out, but I was aware of what he was doing. My hands were tied down and my head was immobilized. I didn't like that feeling and felt fear. My mother was just outside the office and I wanted her in there with me, but I didn't want to appear to be a mother's boy, so I just moaned. The surgeon gave me more valium and went out for a few minutes. Then I was put in the wheelchair and taken out to the waiting room. My mother burst into tears as she saw me and I knew I must look awful. I couldn't talk as they had wired my mouth shut.

"The doctor said I had beautiful teeth, almost too good as there wasn't much room to even take in liquids. But one tooth had been broken in half, giving me just enough space to put a straw. Back in my room, I began to get nervous. The pain was making me crazy, and I couldn't sleep. Then the nurse told us that sometimes if you became sick while your mouth was wired, you could choke to death. Then I was really scared and I could tell my mother was also. She went out and bought some pliers so in case I felt sick once I left the hospital, she could cut those wires out.

"The doctor was mad at the nurse for telling us that, and said that he had never had anyone to do that. He said since I would be having all liquids, that if I was sick, it would be liquid and come out over the teeth. But still I was afraid.

"My mother spent the night in my room and every time I looked up, she was awake, just watching me. It felt comforting to know she was there. I guess everyone feels safe with their mothers when something like this happens. It was decided that I would go home with her, and my wife would come for a few days to be with me.

"It felt like the pain would never go away, and the first night at my mother's, I took too much medicine. I kept going to her room every few minutes and she would talk to me, and let me talk. She called the emergency room and they said that I had taken too much pain medicine from the itchiness I was having but it wasn't a dangerous amount. I kept going out and getting in bed but I couldn't sleep. I kept seeing that gun, hearing those shots being fired at us, and I began sweating and shaking in fear.

"One time, my mother asked if I wanted to lie down on the bed with her and she let me talk. I had to talk about it to get it out of my system. I was afraid if I went to sleep that I wouldn't wake up. I hadn't laid down with my mother in many years since I was a little boy, but I felt safe with her near me. I felt like nothing bad could happen with her there.

"I finally got better, the pain gradually going away. Not completely, but enough so that I could function again. I wanted to get to work, but the man had hired someone else so I would have to go out and look for another job. The bills were piling up, and I didn't know how I was going to pay them. I learned that there was a victim's fund so I sent the papers out hoping they would pay the hospital and the doctors' bills. I didn't have insurance to cover that, and I surely didn't have the money to pay for it.

"When I tried to eat some food, I became sick to my stomach. I felt fear welling up in me as I was sure that I was going to choke to death. I yelled at my mother and she got the clippers. Running to the sink, it began to come up. The doctor was right, it was just liquid, and I felt relief. Now I felt better. The fear of the unknown is terrible and I had passed another hurdle.

"I still feel the anger, and the hatred at those boys who could cause us so much pain and laugh at it. I still feel the pain, the fear, and I have nightmares. The feeling of helplessness, of not being able to fight back, is very traumatic to me and I don't know if it will go away. My life will be different, and I'll be more careful of who I'm around. I won't be so trusting, and I'll carry these scars around forever. I'll never feel completely safe like I had before. I'll never be able to think that nothing will ever happen to me, or that I'm indestructible, because I faced death and I know it can happen. It can happen to me, and it can happen to you. I'm sure that God was watching over me that day and gave me a chance to escape."

Camille Bell

Mother of Murdered Child

"I grew up in Pennsylvania and moved to Atlanta in 1967 with the Civil Rights movement. I met my husband through SNCC, which stands for the Student Nonviolent Coordinating Committee. I was a member also and they were the people who did the original freedom rides. They dissolved in the '70s.

"I married and we had four children, Maria, Johnnathan, Tonia and Yusuf. I lived in the inner city neighborhood of Atlanta as it was close to everything. My husband and I broke up after ten years of marriage and it was hard raising the four children.

"When this whole thing happened, Yusuf was outside playing that day with the other kids. It was a normal day for us and Yusuf came running in and asked if he could go to the store for the lady who lived a couple of doors down. This wasn't unusual for him to do, to go to the store for one or the other of the neighbors. I gave my permission and he left for the store. He went to the store for her, and after leaving the store to come home, he sort of disappeared off the face of the earth. The store clerk remembered him being there because she had kidded him about buying snuff.

"When he hadn't gotten back in an hour, another neighbor and I walked back up to the store to look for him. We didn't see him and we asked a number of people if they remembered seeing him there. They hadn't seen him so we came back to the house.

"I called the police because Yusuf was the type of boy who would go to the store and come right back. He was a very responsible type kid who would do as he was told and not fool around. Had he wanted to go somewhere else, Yusuf would have come home and asked me.

"Now if it had of been Johnnathan who had gone to the store, I wouldn't have worried after an hour because Johnnathan is the type of kid who never comes right back when he's sent on an errand. He's the kind of boy who would get sidetracked by friends, or a football game or anything else that might catch his fancy. So it would have taken a few hours of his being missing before I would have even thought to call the police.

"The policeman who came to investigate the disappearance had seen

14

Yusuf and he remembered him because it had been such a hot day. The temperature was in the nineties and the police department had to start wearing their winter uniforms that day. It was in October and usually it had cooled off by that time, but not this year. He noticed Yusuf walking down the street swinging a stick. He didn't have on shoes or a shirt and so the policeman had thought to himself that this little kid sure looked comfortable and cool. That's why he remembered seeing him.

"The policeman took the report and told us that he'd keep watch as he was on patrol. He wasn't able to file the report until 24 hours after a disappearance of anyone over seven years of age. The thought behind this was if the child had run away or wandered off, perhaps he would come back and wouldn't get a juvenile record."

Unfortunately in this case and in many others, this rule was a problem because nobody would start to look for a missing child until he had been missing for 24 hours.

"Yusuf had not come back after several days and we contacted different people because the police department didn't have the manpower to search. It's not that I'm saying the people in missing persons didn't do all they could do, but there were only four people in missing persons. They had to handle all the crimes against children in Atlanta along with the missing persons."

Because of the murders in Atlanta, and the various other murders around the country the law on missing children was changed. From the mothers of those killed, and John Walsh's efforts, things began to happen. They worked together with the Federal government to get the Missing Children's Act passed.

The Missing Children's Act eliminates the waiting period across the country. It allows parents to add their children's names to a national computer system so that people begin to search for the child almost immediately.

"I guess if you did count the children who were murdered during this time, Yusuf was probably the fourth, but he was the first to get any publicity to where anyone knew there was someone even missing. They had found two bodies of children killed but it had only rated a couple of lines in the newspaper, way in the back. Then another child was found dead while Yusuf was missing.

"No one knew these kids were even missing except the police because there hadn't been any news coverage. These kids who were missing and being found dead were black and also poor, and this made them not very important to the police.

"I felt like my son was alive, that whoever had kidnapped him would bring him back to me. I promised them if they would just bring my son back I wouldn't press any charges. All I wanted was my son safe and sound. I didn't hear from the kidnapper and time went on.

"It was a pretty rough time and we prayed that Yusuf would be found alive. Eighteen days after he disappeared, they found his body in an abandoned school that should have been boarded up but wasn't, about a mile from my house. When the detective came and told me that Yusuf was dead, I went into shock. I couldn't believe that I wouldn't see my son again. My neighbor and friend was with me and she told me that I would have to make it through this thing and she would be there with me.

"We got through the funeral and I found myself doing things automatically. I didn't realize that I was even doing them at the time as I was still in shock and not wanting to believe that my Yusuf would never put his arms around my neck and kiss me, or run in to make a sandwich because he was hungry. I didn't want to believe that I would never see him again. I didn't want to face it but I had to. I don't know what I would have done without my friend Sarah. She was there for me during all this time.

"A couple of months after that other children started disappearing in Atlanta, so I got together with a number of the parents. We tried to figure out what was going on, and we created a support group for all of us. We didn't get help from the police department, or see any investigations being done. We had to go to the police department and tell them what was going on. We told them that we as parents felt the murders might be connected and we felt a task force should be put together. We never got any of that.

"The police treated our children's murders as if they were misdemeanors. That is because our children were poor, and we were black. They chose to ignore murders of those people they didn't feel were important. The police department just didn't respond. The thing that was confusing to me was that the powers that be were also black. I had to feel that the mayor of Atlanta cared about our children—after all, he was black, too. But he didn't.

"In a lot of ways I felt betrayed by the people that I had helped into office. But along the way I learned that power corrupts, no matter what color you are. Finally there were many, many children missing and dead. People were asking why wasn't anything being done about these children being killed. Why weren't the police out there looking and having media coverage?

"The people who receive the death penalty, had they been the victims, are the people whose murder the authorities didn't bother to investigate. If my kid had of been the one who went to the store and killed somebody, they'd of wanted to kill him, but because somebody snatched him off the streets, they didn't even want to investigate.

"Then Williams was arrested for the murders. The families of those children who had been murdered had set up their own investigations. We couldn't depend on the police, so we hired our own investigators. And from that investigation, we have a number of names of people more logical suspects than Wayne Williams. For some of the murders we practically know who killed them and so do the police, and it wasn't Wayne Williams.

"I believe that Wayne is young and dumb and believed that he couldn't be convicted of the murders if he was innocent. When they started to come down on him, instead of doing what any normal person would do, like saying he wanted to see his lawyer, he called a press conference. He did a lot of dumb things that convicted him.

"I have always been against capital punishment in any form. I feel it is wrong in every case. None of us have the right to take the life of another human being because if we're wrong we can't give them back their life. I don't necessarily think of killing someone as punishment. When they're dead, then you're no longer punishing them. You can't punish the dead, and the only one you can punish are the people that love that person you've sentenced to die. That being the case, why would I want to have any mother go through what was hurting me so much? So when I think of capital punishment, I have to think of the families of those you want to kill, cause those are the people you punish when you kill.

"I think if that person ends up in prison and has to live each day just trying to survive, he will think of why he is there, then I feel he is being punished. I feel that the person who killed my son is still free today. I don't feel revenge in the way that you would think I would. I don't want them to kill the person who murdered my child. Just because I don't want him dead doesn't mean I don't want him punished. If you can't give me back my child in life, don't kill in my name."

Pat Bare

Relative of Murder Victim

"Many years ago, my uncle was mugged on the street in Syracuse, New York, on his way to visit one of his brothers. He was so brutally beaten over the head that he suffered severe brain damage and, after several weeks in the hospital, died as a result. The shock and disbelief that we all felt at first gave way to anger, sorrow and a desire for justice.

"My father's rage, my aunt's tears and the sadness and confusion felt by my cousins at this senseless loss of a family loved one were shared by the entire family. My father was the oldest boy in a family of eight children and my uncle was next to him in age and they grew up very close to each other. I remember the many Sunday dinners we ate at his home growing up. His four children were close in age to my sister and I and were our playmates and friends as well as our cousins.

"All of us felt the pain of having to deal with a police investigation and publicity when we should have been dealing with our grief. To pick up the morning paper and read the details of the brutal death of someone close to you is an ordeal no family should have to endure, but it is what all families of murder victims must do at a time when they are most hurting and vulnerable. They are also subjected to prying questions from acquaintances and even from strangers. 'What was he doing there?' 'Did he know his attacker?' Such questions imply that, somehow, the victim was doing something wrong and was responsible for what happened. I wondered at the time why people ask such things. In retrospect, I believe it is because unless the victim did something to provoke the attack, it could happen to any of us. Such questions are born out of fear and denial.

"When my cousins returned to school, they were puzzled as to why many of their friends made no mention of what happened, offered no condolences, or avoided them. It's hard to understand that people feel embarrassment at not knowing what to say and fearing that they will say the wrong thing, so they often avoid talking about the very thing that murder victims' families most want to talk about, the victim.

"A man was arrested for the murder of my uncle, but he was released for lack of evidence when an eyewitness could not make a positive identification. The thing I remember most vividly at that time was a comment made by my aunt, 'I hope now we can put this behind us and try to get on with our lives.' She had been through a long and terrible ordeal and sounded so drained of her usual energy and enthusiasm for life, but she did not express any desire for revenge. I'm sure she knew that no amount of retribution could restore life to her husband.

The years passed and I gave little thought to the question of the death penalty in our society until I read with horror that a man named Gary Gilmore had been shot to death by the State of Utah after a long moratorium on capital punishment in this country. Until that time I believed that we really were progressing morally in the United States. In 1972 the Supreme Court's Furman Decision had brought an end to the practice of state executions and, while I could rationalize that professional criminals and disturbed, even deranged, persons committed murder, I could not rationalize the act of civilized people planning and carrying out the coldblooded killing of another human being for any reason.

"Gilmore's was a suicide execution as he asked to be put to death, but in 1979 the state of Florida electrocuted John Spenkelink and I became actively opposed to the death penalty. A year later, in response to a small article in a newsletter published by the Fellowship for Reconciliation about an organization called the Death Row Support Project, I began corresponding with two men on death rows in Southern states . . . and I began learning everything I could about the death penalty.

"The facts supported my gut reaction that the death penalty is wrong. It is not a deterrent to killing and, in fact, may increase the homicide rate since what a state is actually saying when it takes a life is that sometimes it is necessary and acceptable to kill. States that execute often have higher rates of violent crime than states that do not and when New York had a death penalty, the murder rate rose immediately after every execution, according to a study by Bowers and Pierce of Northeastern University. I was surprised by a study done by the New York State Defender's Association documenting that it is far more costly to execute people than to keep them in prison for life, but was not surprised at statistics showing that the death penalty is racially discriminatory and is used, not for the most heinous crimes as proponents claim, but against those who are the most expendable in our society: the mentally ill, the mentally retarded, the poor, and members of minorities. Neither are our courts infallible, and innocent people have and will continue to die for crimes they did not commit.

"During the past ten years, my opposition to the death penalty has grown so strong that working against it now occupies all of my time. Strangely, it was several years after getting involved in this work before I put together my struggle against the death penalty with the death of my uncle. Only after someone said to me, 'You'd feel differently if it happened to someone in your family,' and I responded with, 'It has and another killing won't bring him back,' did I realize the potential of organizing murder victims' families who felt as I did as spokespersons against state-sanctioned killing and began speaking and writing from this perspective.

"I was surprised by the number of murder victims' families who shared my feelings, though many did not want to speak out publicly for many reasons—some because they wanted to put the incident behind them and involvement was just too painful, others because it is an unpopular position and brings criticism, sometimes even from other family members. I know we are in the minority, but feel this is partly due to public expectations and due to influence from law enforcement, prosecutors and politicians who imply that taking the life of the offender will somehow benefit survivors. In reality, it does just the opposite. It promises victims that another death will make them feel better. It drags the legal process on for years and years during which the crime must be relived every time there is an appeal, and if the offender's sentence is changed the family feels cheated. However, if the offender is executed and the family doesn't feel the relief that has been promised, they also feel cheated. At the same time, a whole new set of victims are created, the family members of the executed.

"I believe it is wrong to kill. It was wrong when my uncle was beaten over the head for a few dollars and it is just as wrong when states kill their citizens. Killing is evil, and when we take human lives as a matter of policy we all buy into that evil, become a part of it, and evil triumphs while we remain victims. The only way we can free ourselves and get on with our lives, as my aunt put it, is by saying 'NO' to further killing. I don't feel it would be a fitting tribute to my uncle's memory to call for the death of another person, not even the person who took his life. I prefer to give him a legacy of life, to say that what happened to him was wrong and to reject killing by refusing to take part in killing. I prefer to respond to my uncle's death by saying 'Don't kill for me.'"

M. Kerry Kennedy

Daughter of Robert Kennedy

"As the daughter of a murder victim, I take special interest in the debate about capital punishment.

"Speaking both as a victim and as an average citizen fearful of crime, I know two things: Murder is a terrible act and needs to be punished severely. But the death penalty is not the answer.

"The Supreme Court had good reasons for striking down the death penalty in 1972. It was biased against blacks. It was biased against the poor. And it was capricious—in the words of Justice Potter Stewart, 'cruel and unusual.'

"Today's death penalty is little different. It remains racially biased. It remains random. And as we know from the recent releases of two wrongly convicted men (in Texas and Florida) it remains unworthy of our trust.

"Perhaps most important of all, the death penalty does nothing to deter crime.

"I was eight years old when my father was murdered, and I remember praying, 'Please God, please don't let them kill the man who killed my father.' I didn't want another person, any person, to die. And I didn't want another family, any family, to experience the grief that my family was experiencing.

"I now work in the field of international human rights, so I know I'm not alone. No other Western democracy likes the death penalty either. All but the United States have abandoned it.

"I'm also pleased to know that my opposition to the death penalty was shared by someone I hold in great esteem: my father, Robert Kennedy.

"'Whenever any American's life is taken by another American unnecessarily,' he wrote, 'whether it is done in the name of the law or in defiance of law . . . the whole nation is degraded.'

"The religious leaders who call us to fight capital punishment are lighting a great torch of conscience. I am grateful for the chance to add my own little light. Add yours too."

Coretta Scott King

Widow of Martin Luther King, Jr.

"I believe that the death penalty is un–Christian, un–American, and unconstitutional. There is overwhelming statistical evidence that the death penalty is racist in its application, but even if the death penalty was not racist I would be firmly opposed to it because the death penalty makes irrevocable any possible miscarriage of justice.

"I also oppose the death penalty because state-sponsored executions set a dehumanizing example of brutality that only encourages violence. Allowing the state to kill its own citizens diminishes our humanity and sets a dangerous and sadistic precedent which is unworthy of a civilized society.

"Although my husband was assassinated and my mother-in-law was murdered, I refuse to accept the cynical judgment that their killers deserve to be executed. To do so would perpetuate the tragic cycle of violence that feeds on itself. It would be a disservice to all that my husband and his mother lived for and believed.

"The death penalty adds to the suffering of the surviving family members and loved ones of victims and offenders alike. For them, revenge and retribution can never produce genuine healing. It can only deprive them of the opportunity for forgiveness and reconciliation that is needed for the healing process.

"We call on all Americans of good will to join us in our movement to put an end to the shameful spectacle of government murdering its own people and to help us create the kind of society in which we can all take pride."

Annie

Sexually Abused Child
(as told by Annie)

"How can I begin to tell this story? A story I can't confirm is true, a story that lurks in the shadows of my mind, too horrifying to remember, too debilitating not to.

"You're not real people . . . you're shadows. I hear the yelling and screaming—things crashing. I hear a door bang open—my door. You pick me up and shake me, screaming obscenities. Of all the things that you could have happen to you, I was the worst. You throw me down. Mom says, 'Don't blame her,' and tucks me in.

"Your anger stops. You look at me with new eyes. I have a purpose. You can use me—for you. You start out slow and easy. You derive great satisfaction from what you're doing. I like pleasing you, and I'm not as afraid you'll hurt me.

"But you hurt me. It doesn't feel right. Something's wrong. It's not me you want. It's what my body can do for you. 'Daddy, please stop. What you're doing is not making me feel good. It's making you feel good. Help me. I'm your little girl, help me.'

"But you don't help. You want me to respond. You're touching my very soul, a soul that belongs to another. I don't want you in my life like this. Please go!

"But you don't go. You stay and try harder and harder to get me to respond. My body wants to. The feelings are intensely pleasurable. But I don't want to give in. I don't want to be yours.

"Mom is oblivious. I hurt day by day. She doesn't notice. Why doesn't she notice? Why won't she help her little girl?

"I stand looking at you. You don't see me and I try to get your attention. You give it, then brush me away. You're safe. You'll stop him from hurting me.

"But you don't. You're distant. I'm distant. I can't feel hurt that you won't help me. I can't feel anything. I love you, but it's disconnected.

"He keeps hurting me. He wants me to hurt him. 'Suck on it,' he says. I can't. He tells me a story, says it's a game. I want to play the game, don't I? I do, but I don't see what this has to do with it. Eventually I do, but what I'm doing doesn't seem like the game we are to be playing.

"I'm not hurting him. He's immensely pleased. He rubs my head and says I'm the most beautiful girl in the world. Soon he pulls away, goes over to the wall, leans against it with his shoulder, then gets very sick. He scares me. He's breathing funny. His face isn't right. Then he's happy. He fixes his pants and goes downstairs.

"He comes up again. His mouth is on my bottom. He's holding my legs. I try to get free. I cry in my heart, 'Daddy, stop, please stop!' He doesn't.

"Mom comes in. Finally he'll stop. Finally she's come to help. She asks what is going on. He tells her something. It's not what happened. She knows that.

"She comes to me. I want her to stop the pain. She throws a blanket on me and calls me something awful. She hates me. It burns in her eyes and she leaves.

"I'm afraid of her. Why does she hate me? Why am I so bad that Dad hurts me and she hates me? I do not feel. I go to sleep.

"'Melba, Melba, you're going to kill her!'

"'The bastard deserved to die. She's filth!'

"I can't breathe. She ridicules me for not being able to breathe. She has my bear in my mouth. She's thrusting it at me asking why I'm not as satisfied with it as a real man.

"My dad's shaking me. Mom's on the floor. I heard a loud slap. He must have hit her.

"'Is she OK?' Mom asks.

"'I think so, she's just scared.'

"'She ought to be!' Mom leaves.

"Dad holds me. I hold him. I don't want him to leave. I don't want him to stay. If I love him, he'll hurt me. If he leaves, I'll die.

"He leaves. My beloved bear is my enemy. He hurts me too. I have no one. No one will help me. No one but me.

"I watch the door. She'll come back. She doesn't. I go to sleep.

"I wake up. I can't go downstairs. When she sees me, she'll kill me. I have to go downstairs. I fear every step. I stand in the kitchen, ready to be killed as soon as she sees me.

"She sees me. She doesn't care. She gives me something to eat. She says to forget the night before, to pretend it never happened. I go play with my toys.

"It never happened. It never happened. I think about how it never happened. Soon I don't have to think anymore.

"I'm outside in the garage. My dad is sorting trash to take to the dump.

Mom comes out and tells me to stay away from him. 'Jesus Christ, what do you think I'm gonna do?' he says. I don't know. But I do stay away from him . . . and her.

"I'm on the swingset. I'm in another world. A world of perfect love. A world where I'm a beautiful creation of a loving person. A person who would never hurt me. A person who put me in a world of hurt.

"Dad comes home. I tense up. He says nothing to me. I feel relieved. He goes into the house. Soon it will be supper and I'll have to go in too.

"I'm outside and I like it outside. I hate the house. It hurts.

"My grandfather is outside. He loves me and calls me his little Annie. He doesn't call me by my real name. My patron saint is St. Ann. He says I should have a Catholic name.

"I want my grandpa. I need him, but he's so far away. He works the fields on foot. I follow him. As long as I don't bother him, I can follow. I want him, but he's so far away.

"I follow him with my eyes when he works the tractor — up and down the fields. He won't hurt me. I need him.

"He hurts my grandma. Mom and Dad talk about her getting beaten when Grandpa is drunk. I'm never to be around him when he's drunk.

"I get a bike. I'm trusted on the road. It feels good to get away from the house. The house hurts. As I look in the yard from the road, I realize the yard hurts too.

"School hurts. I get on the bus and hold inside all the hurt. Sometimes I can't pay attention.

"But I like the church. That doesn't hurt. God is there. That person who loves me is called 'God.'

"I feel safe in church. I want to be there all the time. But I can't. I must go home. I must always go home.

"Home hurts. I have brothers — lots of them. I'm learning to take care of them. I'll never hurt them.

"Mom hurts me. It's my fault she's miserable. It's my fault she hates me. It's my fault she hates me. She looks for ways to hurt me. She feels good when I suffer. She needs for me to suffer. Someday she'll kill me. Then she won't have anyone to hurt — anyone to make her feel better.

"Then she finds a use for me. If she hurts me, I can't help her. She stops hurting me. I watch my brothers and scrub the floors. I wash the dishes.

"Dad leaves. He's not coming back. Now Mom really needs me. I'm in charge. She goes to work.

"My love for God grows. Church has gone beyond a safe place to be. It's the only thing in life that makes sense. It is the sense of my life. School-mates tease me. My love grows stronger.

"I want to leave Mom and marry Jesus. I go to the convent. Mom's happier than I've ever seen her. I want her to stay happy.

"The convent's not for me. There's more than Jesus here. There's rules, regulations and constant work. I can't work. I'm too tired. I hurt too much inside. Jesus gets farther and farther away. I want out. But I can't go home to Mom — she hurts too much. I must go to Dad. He hurts, but not as much as her.

"What do I make of this, this story I've told you in present tense? While you were in your own worlds, you had a child you were slowly destroying. Save for the grace of God, she would be destroyed — if not by your hands, then by her own hands which psychologically were carrying out your wishes.

"How do I feel today? How do I heal from all this? Can I heal from all this?

"I love you both. The first step in healing was to remember. I'm still remembering. What I do remember, I forgive. There's anger, but it's directed against the sickness that drove you. While you were hurting me, I could not express the love I had for you. As I remember, I can feel the pain, share the pain, then love you. The love frees me.

"I have a long way to go. There's so much I don't remember. This is what I do remember and in it I forgive. God grant me the time, security and loving support so I can remember more."

Support and Survival

Parents of Murdered Children

Parents of Murdered Children Inc. (POMC) is the only national agency that specifically seeks to help the survivors of homicide victims and that follows up with supportive family services after the murder of a family member or friend. These services involve participation in a self-help group for the parents and other family members and friends, phone counseling for any family member, counseling through letters, and assisting people in a process of realistic recovery.

The agency also offers ongoing activities such as educational programs with criminal justice agencies, the religious community, and the general public regarding the problems of survivors following the murder of someone near and dear.

Losing a loved one by murder is one of the most difficult experiences anyone ever has to face. Part of what makes it so difficult is that few people know what it's like, and many don't want to talk about it, so they go through the pain relatively alone, wondering if their feelings and reactions are normal and whether they will ever find meaning in life again.

POMC hopes that all survivors of murdered victims will eventually experience a lessening of their pain. It is their belief that it will come sooner if the survivors can share the suffering with others.

Parents of Murdered Children offers to help families cruelly bereaved. No one should have to endure the horror of a loved one's murder. But if you have endured it, or are enduring it; if you still are troubled by any aspect of your loved one's murder, POMC may be able to help.

This self-help group of parents and other survivors has discovered the truth in two principles of all such groups. First, a person who has recovered from a problem can be far more helpful than a professional using only theoretical knowledge. Second, when an individual helps another without charge, both benefit.

When a loved one dies, bereaved families go through intense personal grief. When a child or other family member is murdered, the grief process is complicated by intrusions into the family's grief. Police, lawyers, and other members of the criminal justice system need information, evidence, and testimony. Television and newspapers focus upon the victim and the grieving family.

Sometimes a murder suspect is apprehended, sometimes not. In either case, there is additional pain. Trials and sentencing, preliminary hearings, and postponements force grieving families to face what may seem to be a lack of justice.

POMC provides ongoing emotional support for many parents and family members by phone, by mail, in person, one-to-one, in group meetings, and through literature. The agency will write or phone any survivor with others in the same vicinity who have survived their loved one's homicide and will help any interested parent of a murdered child form a chapter of Parents of Murdered Children and Other Survivors of Homicide Victims in his or her community.

POMC also will communicate with any professional in the fields of law enforcement, mental health, social work, community services, law, criminal justice, medicine, education, religion, and mortuary science who is interested in learning more about survivors of homicide and their problems.

Membership consists of those who have been cruelly bereaved by the murder of their child, family member or any loved one. Parents of Murdered Children depends upon private donations to cover operational expenses, but also seeks some funding help.

The organization has no religious creed or affiliation.

Parents of Murdered Children was founded by Charlotte and Bob Hullinger in Cincinnati, Ohio, in 1978, three months after their daughter Lisa died from injuries inflicted by her former boyfriend.

Father Ken Czillinger, a Roman Catholic priest active in leading support groups for the bereaved, directed them to others whose children had been murdered and met with the group during the first few months.

In their mutual grieving, the parents discovered that by listening to each other, by crying together if they felt like doing so, by understanding how each felt, their grief was lessened.

POMC has formed chapters and established contact people throughout the United States and abroad.

The group starts each meeting with the members' stories, which are a listing of the traditional acts of murder that the public become accustomed to ignoring. This is a group of strong emotions, of people crumbling as they tell their stories, and of people laughing, sharing joys and photos of the living and the deceased.

It is not an easy group to sit in. There are many family members who want only revenge, who are bitter beyond Job's bitterness, who have tasted an experience that has snapped their belief in everything strong, good, and decent.

Yet they continue to continue. The process of discussion branches out to take in new members, who offer help to clergy, the criminal justice system, and others to the methods of humane and loving response.

As parents and other family members who have also survived the violent death of a son, daughter or other loved one, the members of POMC wish to share some thoughts on coping and to offer additional materials that survivors of homicide victims may find helpful.

First, don't be surprised at the strong emotions that come: shock, disbelief, anger toward the murderer, frustration with justice delayed or denied, seeming loss of faith in God and people.

Second, you may feel as if you're going through a nervous breakdown, but you're probably not. You may be confused, depressed, or unable to stop crying. These are normal reactions.

Third, be gentle with yourself and others. Grief takes much longer to work through than most people realize. It affects the body as well as the emotions.

Fourth, as much as you may want to do it, don't build a wall around yourself. It will help your recovery to be involved with people in some way, especially if you can channel your strong emotions into some kind of constructive action.

Parents of Murdered Children
100 East 8th Street, B-41
Cincinnati, Ohio 45202
(513) 721-5683

National Organization for Victim Assistance

After the first cry for help, for most crime victims there is usually a second cry. After the crime, the second cry for help may not be heard. Even by the victims themselves.

"On August 14, 1981, my implicit trust in the goodness of the world ended. On that day, two of my friends were murdered and I escaped death by a fluke."

"I know I'm lucky to be alive; the police told me that 85 percent of rapists use a weapon or threat of physical force. But I don't feel lucky. . . ."

"I feel like I'm going crazy, it was such an unimportant thing. I only lost my stereo and my television. But I keep thinking about how awful it was to come home and find them gone. I can't focus on my work and I don't want to talk to any of my friends. They don't understand. It's just so stupid."

Victims are not crazy or ill. They are normal people who have suffered an intentional act of human cruelty.

And the fact is that victims often need help. In this country, every minute there are 50 thefts, 13 burglaries, and nine assaults. The victims of those crimes may need assistance in replacing their property or paying their bills.

Victims may need medical help. In this country, every day there are 1,400 children abused, 480 women raped, and 55 people murdered. The victims and survivors of those crimes may need emergency help.

In this country, every year millions of victims suffer the loss of trust, the violation of self or home, a threat to their survival. They may need assistance in dealing with the crisis and the short-term or long-term consequences of victimization.

NOVA believes there should be services at every stage of the crisis of crime, from the time the crime happens until after the final sentence of an offender.

The following types of assistance are needed:

1. Emergency response. A set of services to be provided by the first persons coming in contact with the victim after the crime. These services

should ensure the physical safety of the victim and make him or her feel safe and secure.

2. Victim stabilization. These services should follow immediately after the emergency response. They include crisis intervention or other kinds of emotional support following the trauma as well as the provision of protection, shelter, food, or emergency aid.

3. Resource mobilization. Such services are designed to assist the victim in his or her recovery and achievement of a new life. They include a broad variety of help ranging from filling out insurance forms and filing for victim compensation to short-term counseling or long-term therapy. This stage may last for years with some victims.

4. Post arrest. When an arrest is made, a victim automatically becomes involved in the criminal justice system. Services need to be provided to keep him or her informed of the investigation and the arrest, the potential and actual charges which are filed, and any bail considerations.

5. Pre-court appearance. Services at this stage focus on preparing the victim for his or her involvement in the court process. Examples include providing him or her with an orientation to the courthouse and the courtroom, telling him or her what to expect in a hearing or trial, and describing what he or she will be expected to do.

6. Court appearance. Victims who become involved in a court appearance need a number of tangible services — transportation, child care, parking, separation from the accused while waiting for the appearance. Often overlooked is the need for escort and supportive counseling both in courtroom and after the appearance is over.

7. Pre-sentence. More and more states have legislation that allows the victim to be involved in the sentencing process. Services at this stage include assisting the victim with a victim impact statement or alternative expression of his or her concern, escort and support for victims wishing to allocute at the sentencing hearing, and short-term counseling following the sentencing outcome.

8. Post-sentencing. Often the services needed after a sentencing are ignored. Yet victims need to be kept informed about probation revocation hearings, parole hearings, escapes, appeals, and other issues related to the criminal justice system. They also may need continued short-term counseling or long-term therapy now that the case is over.

Many different kinds of programs and individuals can be involved in the delivery of such services. Examples include victim service programs, judges, victim compensation programs, community crisis centers, district attorney offices, self-help groups, rape crisis centers, law enforcement agencies, victim restitution programs, domestic violence shelters, community mental health centers, probation departments, gay and lesbian antiviolence projects, ethnic and racial antiviolence projects, and a growing number of psychological, psychiatric and social workers trained in treating post-traumatic stress disorders.

Responding to the victim's second cry for help is an obligation for us all.

National Organization for Victim Assistance
717 D Street, NW, Suite 200
Washington, DC 20004
(202) 393-NOVA

Victim Service Agency

In a world only too ready to blame and isolate crime victims, the Victim Service Agency helps people in crisis by offering compassion, support, practical assistance and good advice.

VSA's emergency services, counseling and advocacy hasten victims' recovery and help avoid a second victimization. With more than 50 sites across the city, within the reach of every New Yorker, VSA helps victims and the public regain confidence in the criminal justice and social service systems, and works to make those systems more sensitive, responsive, and efficient.

Counseling has been at the heart of VSA's work since the agency's founding in 1978. Trained to understand the psychological dynamics of victimization, VSA staff assist victims of all types of crime, with special programs for battered women, abused elders, sexually abused children, victims of rape and sexual assault, and families of homicide victims.

With programs for street youth, transients and immigrants, the agency acts on the knowledge that poverty, homelessness and prejudice are also forms of victimization.

For a crime victim or witness, going to court can be bewildering and upsetting. The court building itself can seem like a maze of grim corridors. Many victims feel exposed by the courtroom process, open to intimidation and threats by their assailants. To make the criminal justice system more responsive to victims' needs, VSA maintains dozens of court-based services, including reception centers where victims and witnesses can wait in comfort and safety; a computerized notification service that lets victims, witnesses, and police officers know when to appear in court; day-care programs that provide both recreation and counseling for children whose parents must appear in court; a supervised visitation program that allows children to spend time safely with their noncustodial parent; and an experimental reconciliation initiative that brings victims and offenders together to determine appropriate penalties.

And as a way to keep disputes from escalating into violence and ending up in court, VSA runs Mediation Centers in Brooklyn and Queens where trained volunteers help participants resolve their differences by reaching mutually agreeable solutions.

VSA has 11 neighborhood offices that offer counseling; support groups; emergency transportation; advocacy with employers, landlords, and caseworkers; and help applying for crime compensation.

Project SAFE, VSA's lock replacement service, repairs door and window locks without charge.

VSA staff reach out to the community with educational presentations on victim services and crime awareness and prevention.

VSA works with families who are under emotional and economic pressure to prevent both child abuse and foster care placement.

VSA staff, headquartered in four municipal hospitals, accompany victims of rape and domestic violence during medical examinations and police questionings, make phone calls for the victim, arrange for escorted rides and begin a relationship of advocacy that doesn't stop when the victim leaves the hospital.

VSA-coordinated volunteers on Staten Island are on call throughout the night to assist rape and sexual assault victims brought to hospital emergency rooms.

VSA staff provide counseling and advocacy for students who have been victimized at home, in school, or on the street.

VSA counselors conduct classroom presentations and assemblies that educate students about family violence, sexual abuse, and crime prevention.

VSA's school mediation program helps defuse racism and juvenile violence by teaching students to mediate disputes among their peers.

In 1982, VSA merged with Travelers Aid Services (TAS) to form the Metropolitan Assistance Corporation.

Founded in 1905, TAS brings help to homeless adults, adolescents living on the street, and recent immigrants.

Today, TAS operates out of three offices: Times Square, JFK Airport, and Jackson Heights, Queens, and maintains its pioneering Streetwork Project in midtown Manhattan.

Every night, Streetwork staff reach out to street youth on their own turf, on the streets and in the arcades and fast-food joints of Times Square, with information, health services, guidance and help in taking the first steps away from life on the streets.

TAS's Homeward Bound Project helps people in New York's shelter system return to homes outside the City.

TAS's Immigration Services offers answers to questions about immigration laws, advocacy with landlords and employers, and English instruction, as well as services for crime victims.

Operating as an independent agency within the criminal justice and social service systems, VSA is in an ideal position to initiate change. VSA's experience and research have led to new developments in legislation, changes in courtroom, and police procedure, and innovative programs that make the system work better.

Since its founding, vsa has been in the forefront of research and training in the field of victimology.

Recent research has examined the cost of domestic violence in the workplace, the effectiveness of teaching crime prevention, and the extent to which family violence contributes to homelessness.

Vsa's training department has conducted sessions for hospital staff, corrections officers, police officers, teachers and guidance counselors throughout New York.

A training project for police chiefs on the law enforcement response to family violence brought vsa's experience and expertise to 1,000 police executives across the country and produced two award winning films: *Agents of Change* and *Albuquerque Journal.*

With a dedicated and visionary staff of nearly 500, vsa helps more than 120,000 people each year. As it enters its second decade, vsa is more committed than ever to empowering those who have been robbed of power.

Every year, at least 2.1 million American women are physically and or emotionally abused by their husbands or lovers. This abuse is not just a private matter, it is a crime. And if it's ignored, the violence usually gets worse.

For many victims of violent crime, the suffering doesn't stop when the crime is over. Shattering victimizations such as rape, domestic violence, assault and sexual abuse can leave survivors feeling afraid, angry, hopeless, and isolated for months and even years, and can interfere with their relationships, ability to work, and general sense of well-being. Even when you're not the actual victim, when someone close to you has been victimized, or you've witnessed a violent crime, it can feel like your life will never get back to normal.

For many victims, counseling is the key to recovery. Vsa's Crime Victims Center offers the psychological services that can help crime victims heal.

The Streetwork Project reaches out to street youth on their own turf, on the streets. With their dependable, nightly presence in this harsh and difficult world, Streetwork counselors are able to win the trust of these kids and to provide them with information, health services, guidance, support, and the first steps away from life on the streets.

At Streetwork's Drop In Center at 642 10th Avenue, homeless youth can find a safe refuge from the dangers and fast pace of the streets. Equipped with showers and a laundry facility, the Drop In Center is a place where these teenagers can regain some of their dignity and self-esteem.

Victim Service Agency
2 Lafayette Street
New York, New York 10007

Crime Victim Hotline: (212) 577-7777 (24 hours)
Runaway Hotline: (212) 61-YOUTH (24 hours)
Incest Helpline: (212) 227-3000
Immigration Hotline: (212) 899-4000 or (800) 232-0212

Hope for Bereaved Parents

Hope for Bereaved Parents offers support groups and services for those whose loved ones died by accident, illness, murder, or suicide. The initial meeting of Hope for Bereaved was held on December 4, 1978, for parents who had had a child die. In the beginning, the purpose was to establish a support group. The services listed evolved in order to meet the various needs of the bereaved, their families, friends, and the community. These support groups and services have the endorsement of such organizations as the County Medical Society and Funeral Directors of Central New York, as well as pediatric nurses, college professors, community and business leaders, clergy, and counselors.

The help given in such a support group can add greatly to the physical and mental well-being of the grieving and, therefore, to their family and friends. Facts show that unresolved grief may lead to major physical and or emotional problems, absenteeism, alcoholism, marital breakup and suicide.

The purpose of Hope for Bereaved is to offer understanding, coping skills, support, friends, and hope. These services are provided to anyone in need, regardless of religious affiliation. Donations, sale of resources, newsletter subscriptions, and fund-raising projects enable Hope for Bereaved to offer its many services. Newly bereaved are not charged for the newsletter. There is no charge for support meetings, mailed materials, or personal help.

Hope for Bereaved is a not-for-profit organization.

The death of a loved one is very devastating. Most of us are not prepared for the long journey of grief. At first, we don't really believe it. Often by the time that the reality hits us, our friends and relatives think that we are okay and they go back to their busy lives. We may have physical symptoms that we do not understand—sleeplessness, oversleeping, loss or gain of weight, tightness in throat, inability to concentrate, headaches, stomachaches, etc. Often we push down feelings of anger because of the mistaken idea that nice people don't get angry. This pushed down anger is very harmful to us. Various degrees of depression may enter our life and we may think that we are going crazy. This is common. It is important to understand grief, to learn coping skills and to have a determination to survive the loss. Hold on to hope and visit a Hope for Bereaved support group meeting.

What Happens to a Marriage When a Child Dies

The couple that once laughed together, vacationed together, and shared downfalls together suddenly finds at the time of the greatest tragedy in their lives, the time of their greatest need, that each is an individual. They must mourn as individuals. Separately, in the back of each partner's mind, each believed they could lean on each other as they mourned. But it is difficult to lean on someone already doubled over in pain.

One doesn't expect to outlive a child; the fact appears to contradict nature. Funeral directors have observed that often the grief of parents is much more intense than any other kind of grief. The death may be that of a baby, a school-age child, a young adult, or even a child in their middle or senior years. The grief of the surviving parents seems to go on and on.

Some friction is inevitable in any marriage. Friction becomes compounded with the death of a child. It is not easy but it does help to understand the various problems that may arise. Eventually, with time and work, the grief will soften and the marriage survives.

Till death do us part may seem like the end of marriage when one of the spouses dies. It may also be true when a child dies. According to the Society of Compassionate Friends, a 10-year-old self-help organization for bereaved parents, an astounding 70 percent of marriages in which children have died become endangered and end in divorce. Harriet Schiff, author of *The Bereaved Parent,* puts the marriage breakup figure even higher. Some studies, she states, estimate that as many as 90 percent of all bereaved couples are in serious marital difficulty within months after the death of their child. Couples have shared tragedy, disaster, and grief, but these emotions do not necessarily create a tighter bond. Often, instead of holding them together the bond becomes so taut that it snaps. These statistics point out the devastating effect the death of a child can have on parents. They also point out the need to understand what one is experiencing and how important it is to value the marriage.

Severe marital friction in bereaved parents may develop out of ordinary, everyday irritants. Sometimes the trivia can pull a couple apart. Partners lose their patience, their sense of proportion. They hurt so much they have no tolerance. Allowing petty, manageable problems to become gigantic irritants is a major cause of marital breakdown.

Everyone grieves differently, and couples frequently adopt opposite styles. This situation makes it harder for spouses to support or understand each other and requires a great deal of tolerance and respect for differences. However, this variety of grief in couples may allow the family to continue functioning.

Some parents want to change everything while others do not want to disturb anything. One parent may want to put all pictures, mementos and reminders away. The other parent may almost make a shrine of pictures and of the child's room and things.

When one parent is having an up day, he or she resents the partner being down. The reverse is also true; a partner having a down day can't imagine how the other is able to feel so up.

Even something as basic as weather can affect the marriage. The sunny days may bring hope and warmth into one partner's life while the other spouse can't feel happy on such a nice day that the child isn't there to enjoy it. Spouses who don't like the sunny days usually find that the gray, rainy days don't bother them whereas the other spouse's moods match the gray, rainy day.

Another problem is whether to discuss the dead child. Some parents can be at opposite ends about this. One may speak often about the child who died while the other never mentions the child and may even refuse to let the partner speak of the child. Often the happy memories can be discussed by both but not the grief and death.

On the other hand, mutual protectiveness may become a cause of marital friction. Partners may think that telling their spouses how devastated they are feeling would make the spouse feel worse. However, spouses usually do read each other even if nothing is said. It is better to express the pain than to push it down only to have it surface in other ways.

Socializing after the death can be looked at differently. Sometimes one partner will take the attitude, "We shouldn't enjoy ourselves now that our child is dead," whereas the other spouse may seek the opportunity to be with other people. Sometimes a spouse may even refuse to continue having sexual relations. This denial of pleasure with friends or as a couple may have a serious impact on the marriage. Another consideration is that often some family members or friends will distance themselves from the grieving parents, not out of malice but more from not knowing what to say or do. Bereaved people are not always the best company. This isolation from others adds to the marital strain.

It is crucial that bereaved parents recognize their vulnerability and not take their spouses' reactions personally. With the death of a child the nervous system is raw. One experiences deep and often mysterious feelings. It is scary and unnerving. This severe pain or grief brings out the humanness of both parents, enabling them to see both the good and the bad sides of themselves and their mates. The temptation is to dwell on the negative. It is important to recognize the feelings and to see the negative side but then to work on the grief and to concentrate on the positive.

Marriage is challenging at its best, and with the death of a child the ability to love is really tested. By trial and error, in time a couple can learn to grieve together by developing ways of understanding each other's needs more fully and by committing themselves to the re-creation of their marriage.

Hope for Bereaved Parents
1342 Lancaster Avenue
Syracuse, New York 13210
(315) 472-6754

The Compassionate Friends

The Compassionate Friends (TCF) offers friendship and understanding to bereaved parents, having learned that the death of a child has caused a pain that can best be understood fully by another bereaved parent.

Knowing that all need love and support, we reach out as our own grief subsides to those who still feel alone and abandoned.

TCF believes that bereaved parents can help each other toward a positive resolution of their grief. Each parent must find his or her own way through grief. TCF knows that expressing thoughts and feelings is part of the healing process and offers an opportunity for sharing and learning from other bereaved parents. TCF does not offer professional psychotherapy or counseling; the group seeks the cooperation and the support of the professional community but does not depend on it for supervision or formal guidance. Members welcome the opportunity to share with the professional community what they have learned about the needs of bereaved parents.

TCF reaches out to all bereaved parents across artificial barriers of religion, race, economic class, or ethnic group. It espouses no specific religious or philosophical ideology. It supports its activities through voluntary contributions and assesses no dues or fees. TCF does not participate in legislative or political controversy. Members express their individual views on controversial subjects with respect and consideration for those who may disagree.

TCF understands that every bereaved parent has individual needs and rights. There is no correct way to grieve and no preferred solution to the emotional and spiritual dilemmas raised by the death of one's children. Everyone deserves an opportunity to be heard, but no one is compelled to speak. All have the responsibility to listen.

TCF helps bereaved parents primarily through local chapters that have been established to provide sharing groups with an atmosphere of openness and honesty. Local chapters are autonomous in all matters except those affecting other chapters or the organization as a whole. TCF believes that chapters succeed most frequently if there are three or more founders, at least two of whom are a year or more from their loss, and including at least one father and one mother.

TCF chapters belong to their members. What is said at meetings is considered confidential, and what members learn about one another is privileged information. TCF recommends that attendance at meetings by the media, by students, or by other observers be permitted only with prior announcements and with the consent of the chapter members. Some time, of course, must be spent on organizational problems and financial matters, but TCF prefers to keep this to a minimum and out of the regularly scheduled meetings.

TCF chapters are coordinated nationally to extend help to each other and to individual bereaved parents everywhere.

A national office serves the organization by assisting in the development of new chapters, by offering support and consultation to existing chapters, and by responding to bereaved parents where there is no local chapter. It is often easier and more effective to provide program material and educational services by working together at the national or regional level than by working alone.

The organization seeks opportunities to share with society the insights grief has brought so that future bereaved parents may receive needed understanding and support. TCF encourages other family members, especially siblings, to share in the task of mutual support. Members acknowledge their responsibility to support TCF's local and national goals by contributing what they can of their time, their talent, and their resources. This information comes directly from The Compassionate Friends. For more information contact the national office.

The Compassionate Friends
PO Box 3696
Oak Brook, Illinois 60522-3696
(312) 990-0010

Mennonite Central Committee

Mennonite Central Committee U.S. represents the call to meet human need in the United States. Since 1920 Mennonites and Brethren in Christ have been demonstrating through Mennonite Central Committee their conviction that anyone in need anywhere deserves Christ's active compassion. The cooperative relief and service agency has been one vehicle for them to respond, in the name of Christ, to human need without regard to labels such as ally or enemy, Christian or non–Christian, black or white.

But along the road to service in distant places, they have reminded themselves that they dare not walk past the needy nearby. They must aid and walk with the poor, the oppressed, and the neglected as energetically in North America as they do overseas. To love their neighbors as the Gospel teaches, they must be neighbors, people serving others at home.

Although MCC has had programs for mental health, voluntary service and peace witness in the United States since the 1940s, the formation of MCC U.S. in 1980 has meant a more deliberate effort at faithful response to domestic human need. MCC U.S. is a sister organization to MCC (Canada), which has carried a range of domestic programs since 1963.

Some 100 voluntary service workers are at the heart of the MCC U.S. ministry. They work in urban and rural settings and direct services and community development, MCC support services, and advocacy for peace and justice issues. Voluntary service calls for two or more years of sharing a simple lifestyle with other committed Christians while working through local church or community agencies. Often it involves learning to know people of another culture.

In urban settings like Atlanta or rural ones like Appalachia, volunteers in health, nonformal education and social work provide support for community services in neglected areas of American society. In Miami, involvement in social services has focused especially on the needs of Caribbean refugees; in Minneapolis on American Indians.

MCC U.S. has also been an advocate for American Indians, one of the country's most neglected minority groups, by doing research for Louisiana tribes considering application for federal recognition and by providing volunteers to Indian rights organizations in Washington.

Other MCC U.S. workers in Washington help provide a Mennonite witness concerning the draft, militarism, world hunger, domestic agriculture and issues growing out of Mennonite involvement with the poor at home and overseas.

The MCC U.S. Program, while administering voluntary service, also provides resources to Mennonite and Brethren in Christ churches across the United States so that they can work on behalf of urban minorities, undocumented immigrants, refugees in need of sponsorship, victims and offenders, and the aging.

The Office of Urban Ministries, for example, seeks to enhance urban initiatives in community development and to encourage urban minority congregations in their mission. The Office of Criminal Justice is a catalyst for local alternatives to the criminal justice system, and for congregations to apply the Biblical message of peace to relations between offenders and victims. Immigration and refugee concerns are addressed in a variety of ways including advocacy for undocumented aliens in the U.S. and securing sponsors for refugees seeking to start a new life.

The MCC U.S. Peace Section, through contact with conference peace committees and production of peace literature, promotes alternatives to violence in the resolution of human conflict. The section helps coordinate Mennonite and Brethren in Christ response to expressions of militarism raging from draft registration to nuclear arms buildup. It promotes peacemaking from the personal level through its conciliation services network, to the national level through its Washington office.

Four regional organizations, MCC East Coast, MCC Great Lakes, MCC Central States and West Coast MCC, keep the overall MCC organization close and accountable to congregations and district conferences. They interpret MCC programs and solicit resources and personnel.

MCC U.S. provides other support services for MCC's worldwide ministry. Voluntary service workers make up about a quarter of MCC headquarters staff. The material aid department works with regions to collect material contributions of clothing, school supplies, bedding, soap, and food, and it coordinates thrift shop and relief sale activities. An office on hunger, development and justice education shares what MCC is learning about global needs and helps North American Christians find appropriate lifestyles and witness.

MCC U.S. administers the marketing of SELFHELP crafts items that skilled craftspeople in many developing countries produce. It also coordinates Mennonite mental health centers and hospitals, and Mennonite Disaster Service, a grassroots network of volunteers ready to help clean up and rebuild wherever disaster strikes in North America.

For more information on how MCC is being a neighbor in the United States and how you can participate, write to the following address:

Mennonite Central Committee
21 South 12th Street
Akron, Pennsylvania 17501
(717) 859-1151

Women's Self Help Center

The Women's Self Help Center, founded and incorporated in June 1976, is a private, nonprofit, tax-exempt organization governed by a policy-making board of directors.

The primary mission of the center is to reduce the impact and incidence of the abuse of women by providing a crisis hotline, client services, and community education and training.

Paramount to the success of the center is implementation, with clients, of a self-help philosophy to encourage self-determination, self-control, and the desire to pursue positive directions in their lives. In achieving its objectives, the center utilizes trained volunteers in the delivery of services in all program areas, thereby building a salutary atmosphere of women helping women.

Original headquarters of the Women's Self Help Center was a small, second-floor, three-room office located in the 8100 block of Delmar Boulevard in St. Louis County.

After ten years as a homemaker and mother, Louise Bauschard opened the office with two colleagues, both of whom later sought different career directions.

Inspired by a professor at Washington University who awoke a latent but innate concern for women, Louise was determined to participate in the women's movement in a meaningful manner.

The true direction of the new agency, founded originally to share ideas, resources, and options in the women's movement, became abundantly clear when the phones began ringing and the calls were from battered women. The die was cast: the focus of the Women's Self Help Center would be outreach to battered women.

Under the leadership of Virginia Barnes, milestones almost leap-frogged each other. Provisional membership in the United Way of Greater St. Louis was achieved, affiliation with Family and Children's Service of Greater St. Louis became a reality. Service to adult survivors of childhood sexual assault was added to the agency's major concerns.

Events were moving rapidly, and the case load was increasing as battered and abused women began to break the silence in shocking numbers and turned to the Center for refuge, protection, and true help.

The mounting case load, coupled with staff additions and a lack of all-important parking space, pointed up the pressing need for a move from the cramped quarters, and the board of directors took the lead by authorizing a major capital fund-raising drive.

WSHC offers a 24-hour, seven-day-a-week telephone hotline crisis service, staffed round the clock by trained volunteers. There are also crisis intervention services, including followup person-to-person counseling, and group therapy support sessions to provide continuing emotional help to abused women.

A speaker's bureau was established to educate and inform the community about the primary mission of the center.

There is a referral system for emergency needs, temporary housing, legal assistance, and other crisis-related services.

The center also provides training sessions for women interested in becoming volunteers; Justice Outreach services by staff in prisons, legal, and social service settings; and graduate and post-graduate intern training.

A foundation of all programs and services offered by the center is the guiding philosophy of WSHC. The first component of the philosophy is the firm belief that women have the right to live life with dignity and without violence; no woman deserves to be battered, raped, or sexually abused. The second component is the self-help concept, the center's commitment to helping women learn how to help themselves.

Summing up, WSHC reaches out to women with the necessary information and the emotional support, but each woman is encouraged to make her own decisions about her own life. Each woman has a right and the ability to make her own choices; WSHC provides her with the resources and support to enable her to make those choices. Key to the success of the counseling efforts is the supportive, nonjudgmental role played by all counselors in their interaction with clients.

Publication of a book title *Voices Set Free: Battered Women Speak from Prison* is still another highlight of the 10th anniversary of the Women's Self Help Center. A noted St. Louis journalist, Mary Kimbrough, contributed her services in collaborating on the book with Louise Bauschard, whose counseling experiences with imprisoned battered women are chronicled from cover to cover. Proceeds from the sales of the book, after publishing costs, will be allocated to the Legal Defense Fund of the agency.

Women's Self Help Center
2838 Olive Street
St. Louis, Missouri 63103
Office: (314) 531-9100
24-hour: (314) 531-2003

National Victim Center

The National Victim Center is a nonprofit organization founded in 1985 to assist victims of violent crime and to serve the victims' rights movement. The center functions as a national data bank of information about victims' rights and criminal justice issues. It acts as a clearinghouse for information and referral. More than 7,000 organizations are listed in the center's data base, organizations that provide services to victims of violent crime. In addition to its information and referral activities, the center is active in a variety of other programs and services:

The center designs and conducts education and training seminars on various victim-related issues:

Assistance is given to help states establish coalitions of victims' groups as a means of accomplishing service and public policy goals;

A series of self-help educational manuals are prepared to help victims and advocates become successful community organizers;

The center's Library Resource project provides information and guidance to both school and public libraries to improve their collection and retrieval of publications useful to victims and advocates;

Each year the center prepares a Strategies for Action kit to implement effective public education and community awareness campaigns;

A clearinghouse bulletin on exemplary victims' service programs is published twice each year;

The center maintains a legislative data base that includes all victim-related legislation passed in the 50 states;

A crime victims litigation data base contains over 5,000 references of appellate case decisions involving civil suits by victims against perpetrators and third parties whose negligence caused or facilitated the victimization;

An ongoing public awareness campaign alerts news media to victim related issues and identifies local victims groups for follow-up stories in both local and national media.

The center also sponsors several ongoing research projects, including ritualistic child abuse, special libraries projects, head trauma in child abuse victims, ethnoviolence, and the issue of child abuse allegations during custody or visitation disputes.

The National Victim Center's mandate is to provide services and information to more than 18,000 member organizations and individuals throughout the United States and Canada, and to voice their concerns to a number of constituencies about a justice system that too often ignores the plight of victims.

Individual membership dues are $18 a year. This tax deductible membership fee entitles members to receive the quarterly newsletter *Networks,* the quarterly newsletter *Crime, Safety, and You;* access to the most current research in the field of victimology and victim assistance, advance notification of conferences and special events, and reduced rates for training conferences and discounts on publications offered by the center.

According to the U.S. Department of Justice, Bureau of Justice Statistics, one-fourth of the 93 million households in the United States were touched by a crime of violence or theft in 1988, and 5 percent of the nation's households had a member age 12 or older who was the victim of a violent crime.

Five out of six of today's 12-year-olds will be the victim of an attempted or a completed violent crime in their lifetime.

During 1987, more than 3.4 million, or one out of every 53 adults in the United States, were under some form of correctional supervision on a given day.

A victim's life is forever changed after being touched by violence. The way victims look at themselves and those around them will be different. A very normal reaction to victimization is to look for an explanation, to search for a logical explanation of why the violence happened. Unable to rationalize senseless violence, victims often blame themselves, although most are totally blameless. Feelings of guilt are common to crime victims.

All victims of violence, no matter what the offense, share some common reactions: fear, because violent crime strikes suddenly without warning; grief for the things that have been lost, whether they were material things, loved ones lost to homicide, or less tangible things like the sense of privacy and feelings of control over one's life; and intense anger, often directed at oneself, the police, neighbors, family, or friends, rather than at the criminal. Anger that cannot be channeled in a constructive direction causes both physical and psychological injury.

Almost all victims will find themselves using phrases such as "If only I hadn't..." or "What if I had..." People around victims tend to avoid them or the subject of their victimization. Sometimes well-meaning friends, and even some professionals, will fall back to victim blaming in an effort to explain what happened.

Some other emotional reactions to victimization are shock and numbness, denial and disbelief, guilt, loss of control, despair, confusion, inability to function at previously normal levels, increased dependency upon others, isolation, and feelings of vulnerability.

However, becoming a victim doesn't mean you have to stay a victim. There are some positive steps that can be taken to become a survivor, and these same steps can be used by family and friends as they try to deal with victimization. The Victim Center's consultant, Lu Redmond, a clinician who works with crime victims, gives the following advice:

1. You, your family and friends need to be allowed to express feelings of guilt, of shame and stigma. Listen without saying, "You shouldn't feel that way." We feel what we feel; there are no rights or wrongs to our feelings.

2. Recognize we must express our feelings of guilt, the "if only" syndrome, in order to forgive ourselves. It takes repetitive verbalization to recognize our lack of control over the circumstances.

3. Recognize the mind in searching for a reason when you are blaming yourself for what has happened to you. We do not have control over the behavior of others, no matter how much we wish we did.

4. Your sense of personal safety and security has been violated beyond the belief of others. Neighbors, friends, and coworkers are also searching for a reason. Their minds cannot accept that this could also happen to them. They may use emotional distance to protect themselves, or simply may not know what to say or do for you. Tell them what you need.

One normal reaction to crime and victimization is to ignore it and hope it will go away. After a crime has occurred, there is a tendency to hide from the rest of the world to nurse our wounds. The respect for privacy and safety we take for granted has been violated, and it may seem easier to retreat than to fight back.

It's obvious that in America today, the solution to crime cannot be left to the justice system, police, judges, and prison. We must all become involved; practice crime prevention and teach others.

Don't carry your house keys and car keys on the same key ring. Don't put your name on the keys in case you lose them.

Authorized representatives of utility companies are often in uniform; but all of them carry credentials which they must show upon request. If you still have doubts, ask them to wait outside while you call the company they represent to verify their employment.

Don't leave your entry door open or unlocked, even for a short time, picking up the mail, putting garbage on the curb or in the dumpster, or going to the laundry room.

Never leave a note on a mailbox or external door.

If you receive a wrong number call, never give your number. Ask the caller what number he is calling. Never volunteer any personal information.

When riding alone, keep your doors locked and the windows rolled up.

Keep your car in gear when you stop at a red light or signs, construction delays, etc.

Educate yourself about crime prevention and the victim services available in your community. Look in the Yellow Pages under social service organizations to see what's listed there. Call the district attorney's office and ask if they have a Victim Witness Assistance program. If not, they can probably refer you to appropriate human service agencies.

Join or establish a Crime Watch program in your neighborhood. Even in today's busy life, there is time to get to know your neighbors. Your local police department will be able to help you get started.

But it's not enough just to practice crime prevention methods. We must give future generations of Americans tools to promote safety and personal liberty.

Teach your children not to hate. Let your children know, by both word and deed, there are other ways of settling conflicts besides hitting or verbal abuse.

Monitor what your children watch on television and listen to on the radio. Entertainment that glorifies violence teaches our children that it's acceptable behavior.

Practice responsible citizenry. Exercise your right to vote and take the time to learn about the issues and the candidates, especially those relevant to crime and victims.

Get involved! Become a member of the National Victim Center and join our effort to reduce violent crime in America.

National Victim Center
307 West 7th Street, Suite 1001
Fort Worth, Texas 76102
(817) 877-3355

Criminal Injuries
Compensation Fund

Innocent victims of violent crimes are entitled to compensation in Tennessee, and rightly so. Before the Tennessee Legislature passed the Criminal Injury Compensation Act in 1976, victims had to pay all of their own expenses when they were injured because of a criminal act. These expenses included medical and ambulance costs and wages lost because of time off the job.

Tennessee was among the first states in the nation to compensate innocent victims of crime. At present, the state provides for compensation of up to $5,000 for medical expenses, death benefits to survivors, and lost time and disability pay if injuries are serious enough to prevent a person from returning to work. In addition, our state is now providing up to $2,000 in the same types of compensation to persons who are the innocent victims of motor vehicle accidents caused by drunk drivers. Compensation under both programs is payable to the extent that the expenses or losses incurred by the victim are not covered by insurance or some other direct reimbursement.

Of course, the state cannot fully repay a victim for his suffering or a family when the loved one is fatally injured. But the legislature continues to take positive steps toward helping crime victims and their families through such crises.

Any person is entitled to benefits if he suffers bodily injury as an innocent victim of a criminal act within the borders of Tennessee. Surviving dependents of innocent persons who die as a result of criminal acts committed in Tennessee are also entitled to benefits. If there are no surviving dependents, the victim's estate may receive compensation for unreimbursed funeral and burial expenses. Benefits also extend to those innocent persons who sustain bodily injuries or death while attempting to prevent a criminal act or in an effort to apprehend a person suspected of engaging in a criminal act. In addition, persons who suffer injury or death as a result of an accident caused by a drunk driver are eligible for compensation under the Victims of Drunk Drivers Compensation Program.

The victim (or his survivors) must report the crime to the appropriate law enforcement authorities within 48 hours after the crime was committed, unless good cause can be established for not doing so. A written claim for benefits must be filed within one year after the date of the criminal act, unless good cause can be established for not doing so. Claims for compensation filed on or after January 1, 1990, should be filed with the Division of Claims Administration. Assistance in filing for compensation may be obtained from any attorney licensed to practice law in Tennessee. The program will pay for the cost of the attorney, up to 15 percent of the amount awarded to the victim. This amount is paid to the attorney in addition to the amount paid to the victim, so that the victim incurs no cost in receiving compensation. If you need help in obtaining an attorney, please contact either the Tennessee Bar Association or the bar association in your community.

Additional information on the Criminal Injury Compensation Program may be obtained from the district attorney general office in your county or from the State Treasury Department, Division of Claims Administration, 11th Floor, Andrew Jackson Building, Nashville, Tennessee 37219. (615) 741-2734.

Help Our Children Exist

Lois and Ken Robinson have started a support group for parents of those on death row. "Until you've been in this type of situation, it's hard to understand the kind of emotional trauma you go through," Lois says. "It's not just the inmates who are on death row. We're all on death row waiting for the execution. We're all victims in this. The victims of crime aren't the only ones who suffer, and Texas's death row holds more than just the guilty. We know that murder is wrong, and we sympathize with the victims of violent crimes and their families. We're not trying to deny their pain in any way. What we are saying is that execution is not going to bring their loved ones back or act as a deterrent to future crimes.

One of the organization's primary goals is to abolish the death penalty. "Execution is not a cure for murder," she says. "The only hope lies in preventing the crime from happening in the first place. Such prevention could best be accomplished by active programs to treat mental illness, and drug abuse and alcoholic addiction. Those who commit planned murders out of hate don't get the death penalty because their crime isn't committed in connection with another felony. Most of the people convicted of capital crimes are young men who were high on drugs or mentally ill, or both, and who kill because of confusion or panic."

Help Our Children Exist is an issue chapter of CURE. The chapter is made up of death row inmates, their relatives, and others who oppose the death penalty. To become a member, join CURE and indicate that you wish to be a Help Our Children Exist member.

Victims for Victims

Victims for Victims was founded in 1982 by actress Theresa Saldana after recovering from being brutally and almost fatally stabbed. The New York chapter was formed in 1984.

"I was going to an audition for a guest-starring role on a 'Hill Street Blues' episode and was feeling wonderful that morning," Theresa said. "As I left the apartment the sun was shining brightly and I walked to my car which was parked on the street. As I was getting ready to open the car door, I heard a voice calling my name. When I turned around, I saw a man. He reached into a bag and I saw a kitchen knife in his hand, raised above his head. I stared in horror and couldn't move. The knife found its mark and I screamed. He thrust the knife in my body over and over and I screamed, 'He's killing me, he's killing me.' I could sense the people standing around but no one came to my rescue.

"I kicked at the man and tried to block his blows with my arms but I couldn't stop his steady assault. Never in my life will I forget the horror I felt when I stared into his eyes and realized that he intended to kill me. Still no one came to help me. My strength was leaving when suddenly I saw an angel. A tall blond man was standing behind the assailant and in slow motion I saw him pull the man off me.

"I fell to the ground but I had a desperate fear that if I lost consciousness I would surely die. I got to my feet. I somehow found strength to stumble to my apartment. I could see people hiding in fear, watching me bleed to death instead of coming to my aid. Blood was all over my body and just as I was about to fall, my husband ran out from our apartment and caught me in his arms.

"He carried me to the apartment and laid me down on the floor. Then he called the hospital and the police. My lung had collapsed completely, and I was fighting for air. I whispered that I was dying. Fred kept telling me over and over that I would be all right. The pain was so gripping that I prayed for death. I couldn't get a breath of air and my body was in the process of shutting down. Yet I was fighting to survive.

"The ambulance finally came and placed an oxygen mask over my face. They cut most of the clothing from my body and relayed the information back to Cedars-Sinai Hospital. There were 10 separate wounds. They put me in a trauma suit, a pair of rubberlike pants, which when inflated would force the blood from my legs to the vital organs.

"Every inch of my flesh cried out in agony; I was afraid that the pain would kill me, but I clung to life, fighting to remain conscious. I had never known such pain existed and I screamed.

"By early April, I was to be released from the hospital. I had to face the problem of where I would go from there. I would need continued care and treatment, and I found that my insurance wouldn't cover it. It was decided that I would go to the Motion Picture and Television Fund Hospital in Calabasas.

"I was afraid of being alone and needed someone with me at all times. My parents had been there but they needed to get on with their own lives now. My father and sister went back home, but my mother stayed on to be with me.

"My husband Fred and I had been growing apart steadily and it wasn't long before we broke up. He told me later of his feelings of people ignoring his pain and concentrating only on mine. Our entire family had been victims of this cruel man. I felt isolated and alienated and I even referred to myself as a freak. Physical therapy was excruciating but I knew that I would have to endure the pain if I wanted to get better.

"It was while I was on a pass from the hospital that I met Miriam Schneider, also a crime victim. She had lived through a nightmare of physical and emotional pain, and we found a lot to talk about. It was that day that I formulated the idea for Victims for Victims, an organization where victims could reach out to one another. Victims for Victims would not hold its first formal meeting for six months, but it was already very real in my mind.

"I was having flashbacks and heard the attacker's voice, saw the blade glinting in the sunlight, and felt the knife being plunged into my body. For a long time after the attack fear ruled my life. Sometimes I couldn't even go down the hospital corridor, and it almost paralyzed me.

"Without the help of my psychiatrist, it would have been nearly impossible for me to get through the summer and fall following my attack. The anger that engulfed me made me feel like a walking time bomb. I truly believe that despite the horror of our experiences, those of us who have been victimized can fight our way back through the pain, the fear, and the anger, to a joyous, fulfilling life beyond survival."

Victims for Victims offers telephone support, group sessions, and referrals to victims of violent assaults, including rape, mugging, stabbing, and hit-and-run accidents. All Victims for Victims personnel are trained by professional psychotherapists from the Rape Crisis Center at Cedars-Sinai Medical Center.

Victims for Victims works with city, state, and volunteer groups, including the Victim Services Agency, the Crime Victims Compensation Board, and the National Victim Center.

Victims for Victims, along with other grassroots organizations in the New York area, is also pressing for tougher crime laws and a victims' rights amendment.

Victims for Victims is funded by donations and membership dues.

"I thought I was going crazy," said one stabbing victim. "I was scared to be in my apartment. I was scared to go out of the apartment. I couldn't sleep without all the lights on. Then I went to the support group and I heard everyone else say the same thing. Talking to the other victims who were struggling and a group leader who had already recovered helped me to see that I wasn't losing my mind and to eventually recover some of my lost sense of security. I don't walk down the street with the same confidence I once had, but I'm out there again walking."

A gang rape victim adds further testimony: "There is no better way to deal with the torture of rape except getting it out to people you trust; being able to say things other people wouldn't understand. To watch the healing process is the most amazing miracle you could ever experience."

New York Governor Mario Cuomo may have been overstating the matter when he said that "No one is safe," but certainly the streets are no longer a place to walk without worry of attack. The case of the Salomon Brothers associate who was assaulted, raped, and left for dead by a gang of teenagers is unusual only in its brutality. Every day scores of New Yorkers are raped, stabbed, beaten, and held up at gunpoint.

For those who survive, the ordeal has only begun. Not surprisingly, the emotional wounds are usually as deep as the physical ones. For months, even years after the assault, most victims are afraid to do things other New Yorkers take for granted. Regardless of how and where they were attacked, recent victims are often afraid to be alone in their apartments or to leave without an escort. After those fears have eased, many find that they cannot travel in a taxi with only the driver or ride in an elevator with passengers they do not know.

Although ample state funds are available for the care and rehabilitation of offenders, victims are left to fend for themselves. Therapists agree that peer support is the most effective way for a victim to get past those fears and resume a normal life. Yet Victims for Victims is the only organization in New York that provides peer support to victims of all violent assaults. Victims for Victims now offers weekly peer groups in lower Manhattan and Brooklyn and hopes to expand to Queens by the mid–1990s. Its goal is to have a support group in all five boroughs. Victims for Victims provides transportation assistance home from group sessions for victims who are too traumatized to return home via public transportation. Victims for Victims also offers telephone support sessions for victims who are unable to attend group sessions or who need additional support.

Over the course of a year, more than 200 victims attend at least one group session. Recent participants include a woman who was stabbed while jogging, a man who was held up at gunpoint and in the course of defending himself killed his attacker, a woman who was gang-raped by a dozen neighborhood youths, a woman who was dragged by a car down a Bronx street after the man in the passenger seat grabbed the camera that was strapped to her neck, a man who lost his legs when a mugger pushed him off a subway platform onto the tracks, and a woman who was raped at gunpoint after watching her assailant shoot and kill her husband and her sister. Group leader Nandrea Linn Courts was almost killed by a hit-and-run driver in 1986.

Victims for Victims helps victims to solve legal questions arising from their assault and provides guidance in dealing with the Victim Service Agency and the Crime Victims Compensation Board. Victims for Victims refers cases involving battered women, child abuse, and ongoing family abuse to other agencies.

Victims for Victims also can provide limited financial assistance to victims facing a financial crisis because they are unable to work; Victims for Victims is developing a program to provide volunteer escorts to recent victims who cannot otherwise leave their homes alone. The biggest problem facing most assault victims is the overriding fear that they will be attacked again; for many the answer is to flee, living with friends or family while they put their lives back together. Victims for Victims hopes eventually to open a safe house in Manhattan where recent victims and victims awaiting parole release of their offender may reside for short terms in relative safety until they are able to return home.

Victims for Victims
P.O. Box 5966
Grand Central Station
New York, New York 10163
(212) 431-1200

Victims Outreach

Victims Outreach is a recovery and advocacy program for victims of violent crime. Its members are all victims.

A violent crime is reported in Texas every five minutes. More than 50 percent of violent crime goes unreported. Only 11 percent of reported violent crimes result in the incarceration of the perpetrator. The average violent criminal in Texas serves only one-fifth of his sentence before being released. Five out of six of today's 12-year-olds will be victims of violent crimes in their lifetime. About half of those will be victims two or more times.

The cost of the criminal justice system exceeds $45.6 billion per year. Yearly losses from personal and household crime exceed $13 billion. Each year $665 million in tax money is spent on defense attorneys for indigent defendants. Total financial losses due to crime exceed $50 billion per year.

The Plight of the Victim

Excerpts from the statement of Lois H. Herrington, chairman of the President's Task Force on Victims of Crime:

Something insidious has happened in America; crime has made victims of us all. . . . Every citizen of this country is more impoverished, less free, more fearful and less safe, because of the ever present threat of the criminal. Rather than alter a system that has proven itself incapable of dealing with crime, society has altered itself.

When victims come forward . . . they find little protection. They discover instead that they will be treated as appendages of a system appallingly out of balance. . . . The system has lost track of the simple truth that it is supposed to be fair and to protect those who obey the law while punishing those who break it. Somewhere along the way, the system began to serve lawyers and judges and defendants, treating the victim with institutionalized disinterest.

The President . . . recognized that in the past these victims have pleaded for justice and their pleas have gone unheeded. They have needed help and their needs have gone unattended. The neglect of crime victims is a national disgrace.

You must know what it is to have your life wrenched and broken to realize that you will never really be the same. Then you must experience what it means to survive, only to be blamed and used and ignored by those you thought were there to help you. Only when you are willing to confront all these things will you understand what victimization means.

Victims Outreach is a nonprofit corporation that provides a wide range of services to the victims of violent crimes, their families and friends.

For those people in Dallas and surrounding areas, Victims Outreach supports and guides emotional healing, eases passage through the complexities of the criminal justice system, helps victims find solutions to other problems in their lives caused by violent crime, and increases public awareness of and sensitivity to the needs of victims and survivors.

The organization provides emotional support by offering information on grief and overcoming victimization, 24-hour telephone support, peer group support meetings, and group debriefings when violence occurs on the job or at school.

Victims Outreach also provides criminal justice support in the form of information on the criminal justice system and victims' rights; liaisons with law enforcement and prosecuting agencies; support and assistance through investigation, trial, appeals and parole; and accompaniment to court during trial.

Other support services include help with crime victim compensation; employer, landlord, and other intervention services; contact with other state and national victims' groups; referrals to other appropriate agencies; and a lending library.

Victims Outreach promotes public awareness through in-service training, sensitivity training, information on victims' and criminal justice issues, and a speakers bureau.

The tragedy of crime doesn't end with the criminal incident. Nonviolent crime may affect victims for a relatively short period of time. Victims of violent crime will be forever changed.

It takes six months for the victim of a violent crime to recover. If the victim is permanently crippled, loses a large percentage of his property or financial worth, or loses a loved one as a result of the crime, it may take two years or more to stabilize, and several more to heal. Some never recover.

Victims Outreach
P.O. Box 515727
Dallas, Texas 75251-5727
(214) 233-5184

Project Hope

Project Hope is a group of inmates, concerned citizens and supporters working with family members, friends, and other advocates nationally to attempt to influence public opinion regarding capital punishment through education in an effort to abolish the death penalty.

Thus far in an effort to educate and build a community of sympathetic supporters, the group has been distributing project materials to Holman Inmate family and friends, — a smattering of people across the country, faith community, legislators, educators, news media, etc.

With so many misconceptions about the death penalty, the real key is to educate . . . to communicate all the facts, the whole truth concerning capital punishment. That's really, by the grace of God, the desired and hoped for purpose of Project Hope — through education to have a positive influence on public opinion, breaking down the varied and multiple walls of resistance through speaking the truth in love, out of a spirit of love and caring, compassion for wounded, scarred, and suffering humanity . . . suffering at the hands of whatever the injustice.

Project Hope is in the process of establishing support groups within its chapters to help family members understand the true essence of the death penalty and all it stands for.

Members also hope to establish communication between family members and advocates who in the future will be able to share and help one another in times of need for purposes of transportation sharing on occasions of out-of-state visiting, and all other general support group sharing.

The organization has established its project headquarters in a nonkilling state. It plans, however, to establish satellite groups in Alabama as well as other states representative of those individuals condemned to death row in Alabama. Project Hope's leadership plans to organize and establish a foundation and platform by unifying its position with all concerned members of society who believe the death penalty is a savage, brutal, and unjust punishment.

Project Hope asks all family members, friends, or any member of society supporting the destruction of state-authorized murder to write and offer your support by giving your name, address, and zip code to the organization's national directory so that Project Hope can share its material with you, especially that regarding progress, news information and programs the organization intends to establish on behalf of the fight against the death penalty.

"Would Jesus pull the lever that would kill someone or would he inject their arms with poison? Neither would I."

Project Hope
P.O. Box 36386
Birmingham, Alabama 35236

Project Hope
P.O. Box 8121
Oshkosh, Wisconsin 54901

National Clearinghouse for the Defense of Battered Women

The National Clearinghouse for the Defense of Battered Women (NCDBW), created in the summer of 1987, provides critical assistance, resources, and support to battered women who have killed or assaulted their abusers while attempting to protect themselves against brutal and life-threatening violence, and to other battered women who have been coerced into crime by their abusers. The Clearinghouse offers direct technical assistance to defense teams nationally, maintains a comprehensive resource bank, provides direct support to battered women in prisons, coordinates a national network of advocates working with women in prison, and provides community and professional training seminars. All of these efforts serve to enhance the quality of legal representation and personal support to battered women defendants by building bridges and alliances between the battered women's movement, the criminal defense bar, social scientists, and others concerned about domestic violence. If you are currently working with a woman who is facing criminal charges or is currently incarcerated call the National Clearinghouse for assistance and information.

The Clearinghouse maintains a resource library that contains more than 1,400 up-to-date cases and articles relating to battered women defendants and their legal defense. These materials in their library are available for $25. This listing is a must for anyone working with battered women defendants. A 40-page statistics packet about partner homicide and battered women in prison is also available.

Battered women who are charged with killing or assaulting their abusive partners are being vigorously prosecuted. Ironically, despite heightened public sensitivity to domestic violence and its victims, many battered women who have acted in self-defense are being convicted and sentenced to harsh jail terms. This trend is particularly true for women of color and women of low income. Studies suggest that as many as eight out of ten battered women charged with killing their abusers are convicted or accept a plea to some charge. Any understanding of a battered woman's victimization is often lost when she becomes a defendant in a criminal case.

If you have worked with a battered woman defendant in the past,

Clearinghouse staff members are eager to speak with you about your experiences. They are collecting information from attorneys, advocates, expert witnesses, and battered women from across the country to help better understand advocacy and defense strategies that are most helpful to battered women defendants . . . on both a legal and emotional level.

At the National Coalition Against Domestic Violence national conference in July 1988, women interested in organizing the network put in some long, hard hours of work in between workshops. On the last day of the conference, they submitted the following resolution at the membership:

"Whereas, battered women fill the jails and prisons of this country and

"Whereas, their voices are often not heard and their needs remain unmet and

"Whereas, the inherent racism and class oppression of the criminal justice system results in a disproportionate number of women of color and low income women being incarcerated and

"Whereas, battered women who are arrested, prosecuted, convicted, and incarcerated rarely receive necessary advocacy and support services they need in their search for justice and freedom,

"We urge the NCADV and its active member agencies to understand the many complex issues involved in working with currently and formerly incarcerated battered women and

"We urge the NCADV to make advocacy efforts on behalf of battered women who are, were, or may be incarcerated a national priority."

The network is looking for new members and additional resources. If you are interested in working on any of the projects, contact:

The Network c/o NCDBW
125 S. 9 Street, Suite 302
Philadelphia, Pennsylvania 19107
(215) 351-0010

On Dealing with a Violent Death

by Father Kenneth Czillinger

Generally it takes 18 to 24 months just to stabilize after the death of a family member. It can take much longer when the death was a violent one. Recognize the length of the mourning process. Beware of developing unrealistic expectations of yourself.

Your worst times usually are not at the moment a tragic event takes place. Then you're in a state of shock or numbness. Often you slide into the pits four to seven months after the event. Strangely, when you're in the pits and tempted to despair, this may be the time when most people expect you to be over your loss.

When people ask you how you're doing, don't always say, "Fine." Let some people know how terrible you feel.

Talking with a true friend or with others who've been there and survived can be very helpful. Those who've been there speak your language. Only they can really say, "I know; I understand." You are not alone.

Often depression is a cover for anger. Learn to find appropriate ways to release your suppressed anger. What you're going through seems so unfair and unjust.

Take time to lament, to experience being a victim. It may be necessary to spend some time feeling sorry for yourself. Pity parties sometimes are necessary and can be therapeutic.

It's all right to cry, to question, to be weak. Beware of allowing yourself to be put on a pedestal by others who tell you what an inspiration you are because of your strength and your ability to cope so well. If they only knew.

Remember you may be a rookie at the experience you're going through. This is probably the first violent death you've coped with. You're new at this, and you don't know what to do or how to act. You need help.

Reach out and try to help others in some small ways. This little step forward may help prevent you from dwelling on yourself.

Many times of crisis ultimately can become times of opportunity. Mysteriously your faith in yourself, in others, in God can be deepened through crisis. Seek out persons who can serve as symbols of hope to you.

Surviving When Someone You Love Was Murdered

by Lula Redmond

"Grief is the kernel of all psychopathology." This profound statement was made by Norman Paul at the International Conference on Grief and Bereavement in London, England. If one can accept that grief is the seed of psychopathology, we can understand the importance of going through the mourning process and accomplishing a healthy resolution to our losses. This becomes the very basis of sound preventive mental health care.

The process of resolving conflicts imposed on us by death is called mourning. Bowlby and Parkes provide four helpful descriptive phases of the mourning process: 1) shock and numbness; 2) yearning and searching; 3) disorientation and disorganization; and 4) resolution and reorganization.

All four dimensions are usually present when the mourner learns of the death. There is an ebb and flow, highs and lows in the process; there are no neat dividing lines between the characteristics. As the mourner begins to resolve conflicts of the loss, feelings of shock and numbness pass, there is less searching and yearning, disorientation and disorganization appear less frequently, and the mourner reorganizes to learn how to relate to the world without the deceased. It is the resolution of the conflicts brought on by the death, not the passage of time, by which the mourner achieves resolution of the process. Time alone does not heal. For those who avoid grief work, time does nothing but pass, leaving grievers to deal with unresolved, delayed grief reactions which may become exaggerated and complicated. However, it takes time to resolve the many changes in one's life brought on by the death of a loved one. Grief work may dominate the life of a mourner for the first two years following a death.

Immediately upon news of the death, the mourner feels stunned; there may be outbursts of intense panic, distress, and anger directed toward those present. Functioning is impeded. Decision-making is difficult and concentration is limited. A protective psychological numbing occurs as the defense mechanisms of denial protect the ego. Mourners describe feeling as though they are encapsulated within a heavy plastic shield, observing others in an unreal world. The mourner remains distant from others, feels vulnerable, and is protective of self. When the psychological shock is so severe as occurs in unexpected deaths (accidents, suicide and homicide), there may be no memory of what was said or done. There is loss of emotional connection within the mourner, and between the griever and the outside world. Attention span is short at the time when crucial, objective decisions must be made, such as funeral arrangements and estate settlements. Characteristics of shock and numbness appear to be most intense in the first two weeks but may peak again on the anniversary of the death or at other trigger points in the life of the bereaved.

The mourner may have the fear of going crazy, as one hears, sees, or senses the presence of the deceased. The mourner is sensitive to the habitual sounds and sights associated with the deceased's car pulling into the driveway, sounds of the key in the door latch at the usual homecoming time of day, or seeing the deceased in a crowd at a mall. Even feeling the hand of the deceased on a shoulder may be normally described during this period. The mourner may forgetfully set a place at the dinner table, then hurriedly remove the setting for fear of being discovered by other family members and being regarded as emotionally ill. One fears for one's own sanity. The mourner may be overwhelmed with feelings of anger, self blame, and guilt. Davidson explains that during this period the mourner is testing what is real. Equilibrium cannot be restored until reality is established and understood. Searching and yearning behaviors appear to be most intense from two weeks to four months following the death, but may reappear around the anniversary.

The mourner feels disorganized, depressed, guilty, and unable to accomplish normal tasks. Disorientation appears most intense from the fourth to sixth month following the death. By this time friends, other family members, and co-workers may voice the expectation that the mourner should be over the acute grief. The opposite is true. The mourner feels more pressure from the expectations of others, while at the same time experiences heightened anxiety over an inability to organize thoughts and actions.

This is a time the mourner most needs the support of others. Physical symptoms of stress appear. Complaints may vary from cold symptoms, flu, tiredness, and insomnia to a range of psychosomatic illnesses. Physicians without a careful assessment may diagnose the symptoms as clinical depression, rather than part of the mourning process. Contrary to popular opinion, antidepressants and tranquilizers are not appropriate for treatment except in rare circumstances. These drugs may mask the symptoms and lead to a long-term unresolved grief reaction.

When the death occurs from sudden, unexpected circumstances such as a heart attack, accidents, suicide, or murder, bereavement reactions may be more severe, exaggerated, and complicated. The coping mechanisms of the mourner may be overwhelmed. This is not meant to indicate that grief is not painful regardless of the type of death, or that one bereavement reaction is more severe than another, but rather that other factors may impinge leading to a more complicated bereavement.

There are varied reasons for the delayed, exaggerated, and complicated bereavement reactions experienced by survivors of homicide. Major characteristics experienced by survivors are cognitive dissonance, disbelief and murderous impulses, conflict of values and belief system, and withdrawal of support due to the stigma of murder. Survivors must deal with feelings of fear, vulnerability, anger, rage, shame, blame and guilt, and emotional withdrawal. The lack of familiarity with support by law enforcement, the criminal justice system, and media intrusion also lead to bereavement complications. The delays in resolution of the murder conviction, lack of adequate punishment for the crime, and the lack of acknowledgment by society heighten the feelings of loss of control.

At news when someone you loved was murdered, the first reactions of disbelief, shock, and numbness are apparent in the inability to accept the news as real. Remarks such as "It can't be," "Oh, my God, no," are indicative of the denial mechanism. There may be claims that the informer must have made a mistake, denying that this could happen to a loved one. There is no preparation for this sudden onslaught. There is no comprehension that death could come so swiftly, and in a violent, degrading, brutal manner at the hands of another human being.

The death does not make sense; the mind cannot comprehend the meaning. The mind demands more information than can be processed or stored. Questions about events leading up to the murder will be asked repetitively, seeking both understanding and confirmation that is not true. Nothing in our coping mechanisms prepares us for this level of psychological trauma.

An example is the case of Jim, who had been part of the search party looking for his missing 14-year-old daughter for over 24 hours. The fire department discovered her mutilated body in a burning shack. Months later, after the funeral, investigations, arrests, and pretrial hearings, Jim continued searching. He circled the same locations covered in the original search. He cognitively knew that his daughter was dead, but "could not believe that she was really gone."

The mind is overloaded with the events prior to, during, and after the murder. There is a constant rehearsal of events: what happened, when, how, who did what, and the unanswerable, but *why?* There may be questions that have been answered in a logical sequence by law enforcement officers, victims' advocates and other officials. None of the answers are good enough. The mind is searching to understand something that is incomprehensible. The act of reordering the events in order to understand takes much longer than we may expect. This cognitive dissonance may continue for months or years, and may be triggered by the court proceedings or other events relating to the murder for years in the form of a delayed grief reaction.

One of the most difficult emotional reactions for survivors, family members, friends, therapists, and others who serve the victimized survivors to understand is the intensity, duration and frequency of anger and rage. Anger is a normal, healthy emotion. Lifton (1979) describes the paradigm of the emotional state of anger on a continuum from anger to rage to violence. To fantasize acting out rage is normal. To act out rage is violent behavior and must be prevented.

For the homicide survivor, the normal anger of grief is compounded by the rage and desire to violently destroy the murderer of the loved one. The psyche is dominated by images of what the survivors would, could, and should do to the murderer. Elaborate plans of torturous treatment may be devised. The images of seeing the murderer suffer in a more horrendous manner than one's own loved one suffered are normal reactions for the murder victim's survivors.

Frequently the survivor is ashamed to tell anyone of the horror of the retaliatory thoughts. It is not unusual for the victimized survivor to fantasize painful castration of a rapist murderer followed by a slow bleeding death. Lifton (1979) explained that anger has to do with an internal struggle to assert vitality by attacking the other rather than the self in order to prevent a sense of inner deadness.

Survivors are frightened by their murderous impulses and their sense of rage. They ask themselves, "Am I no better than the one who killed my loved one? If I know myself to be a good person, yet I feel the desire to castrate, mutilate, or degrade another human being, can I really be a good person?" "If I could do such harm or think of such savagery, am I safe around my own family?" This can lead to emotional withdrawal and deep depression. "I must be going crazy" is the common response of survivors. The survivor should be reassured that he is not "going crazy," that such retaliatory thinking is quite typical and expected under the circumstances. The internal conflict with one's own sense of values, beliefs, and sense of justice is overwhelming. The murderous impulses to attack the other in retaliation for the pain suffered by the murder victim, and the pain of grief of survivors must be explored, exposed, and understood during the therapy process.

It is in venting and verbalizing the murderous impulses that the anger begins to lose some of its intensity and power. The thoughts do not have to be acted out when one can tell the fantasy and the therapist listens with acknowledgment, understanding, and nonjudgmental acceptance.

Verbalization and ventilation provides a path to reframe the scenario; it is a way to rehearse what in effect could, should, and would be done.

It is not unusual to see survivors displace anger. The anger may not be directed at the criminal, but at others who surround homicide survivors. Targets of this displaced anger may be family members, friends, co-workers, strangers in the street or even those who are trying to assist. The threshold level of instant irritation and self-control is low, and survivors do not have the internal controls to endure even slight irritations.

In a stranger-to-stranger crime, the survivor and defendants have little to no contact. Anger, pain, fear, and violation become more real when the offender is caught and brought to trial. Survivors at the trial are amazed at their own restraint. They must endure the pain of seeing this human being face to face. In contrast, if the offender is never apprehended, he or she becomes a mystical figure, elusive and not entirely real to the survivor. There is greater cognitive dissonance because there are more unanswered questions to internalize. Questions which can only be answered in the imagination.

In therapy groups survivors are asked, "What do you want to do with your anger?" It is the survivors' emotion and has the powerful ability to transform negative trauma into positive accomplishment, but the choice must be up to them. This technique is not useful until the anger has been verbalized, explored, reframed, rehearsed, and exhausted. It must be the survivor's choice whether it will be part of an internal dialogue for the rest of his life. Offering the survivor this choice in decision-making adds to a sense of being in control and reaffirms one's power.

In our society, we have held the belief that those who are murdered have in some way led to their own death. Members of a community in which a brutal murder has taken place will often blame the victim or survivors. This is again the same search for a reason to be able to comprehend the horror. By these explanations, a protective shield is set up within the mind of the observer that the circumstances are such that the tragedy would never have happened to them. Everyone is, in reality, vulnerable to victimization but will seek security in finding components of the criminal activity that could never occur in their life. A superficial aura of personal security is established to counteract this real vulnerability.

An internalized sense of personal security is exhibited by onlookers as victims are labeled "bad," "drugged," "careless," "seductive," "promiscuous," "with the wrong crowd," or in some manner "asking for it." Families of victims are also stigmatized because it is believed that they should have stopped the behaviors blamed on the victims, or at least have expected the traumatic outcome. It is as though what is being said or thought is, "If I blame you for letting your child be killed, how can I still be your friend?"

This is irrational thinking on the part of others to prevent acknowledgment of their own vulnerability and the randomness of murder. Evidence of this fact is reflected when it is the murder of an innocent child or an elderly woman or gentleman.

In order to prevent our own loss of control and gain understanding, we project blame on the lack of parental care, other caregivers, or the system within which the victim was a member. The mind continues to search for explanations until it becomes accommodated. In this projection of blame, the observer finds comfort and accepts that one's family is exempt from such a horrendous tragedy. This type of rationale provides emotional distance and exclusion, protecting those who are neighbors, friends, co-workers, and other community members. This type of thinking and reactive behavior by others leaves the survivors alone in their sorrow.

It is the emotional distancing of others and stigmatization that leaves the survivors of homicide feeling abandoned, ashamed, powerless, and vulnerable. Survivors report not receiving sympathy cards, the inability of others even to say "I'm sorry," or co-workers' inability to acknowledge absence from days of work. Examples of these types of sensitivity to the needs of others are acknowledged freely in other types of deaths. Survivors report the sound of whispers among co-workers, recognition that the murder case is the subject, but lack of acknowledgment that it is their murdered loved one under discussion. Friends, who do not know what to say or do, become uncomfortable and withdraw emotional support. Many survivors report that cherished friendships become dissolved at the time of murder of their loved one.

When the surviving family members acknowledge that there were predisposed circumstances, such as drug abuse, which may have led to the murder, this does not lessen the intensity of the loss to the survivor. Those who have opposed parental or spousal wishes do not deserve to be murdered. The survivor must subsequently endure not only the loss of the loved one, but the death of personal hopes, dreams, and unfulfilled expectations that perhaps someday the son, daughter, or spouse would have functioned in a more productive lifestyle. The survivor experiences a greater sense of personal failure when there is ambivalence in the relationship, and the process of bereavement becomes more exaggerated and complicated.

A major goal of therapy is to build a bridge back to the world of the living, recreating a sense of interdependency, so that survivors may reconnect with their families and community. One cannot accomplish this goal without integration of the experience into one's own psychic framework.

Lula M. Redmond, R.N., M.S., is a family therapist in private practice who specializes in the area of unresolved grief. Her concerted efforts are directed at the prevention of mental illness by assisting the bereaved to work through the painful experiences of normal grief. She is an educational consultant for Hospice Programs throughout the country and lectures nationally as a faculty member with the Forum for Death Education and Counseling, Inc. She is founder and president of the West Coast Florida Chapter of the Forum of the Board of Directors of the Mental Health Association of Pinellas County, Inc. Lula Redmond may be contacted at P.O. Box 6201, Clearwater, Florida 33518.

Part II:
Victims of Punishment

Personal Accounts

Shirley Dicks
Mother of Death Row Inmate

"I remember the day I got a call from my oldest son, Jeff, who lived in Kingsport, Tennessee, with his wife, Betty. He sounded scared and asked me to come to Tennessee to pick them up, saying he would tell me what it was all about when I got there. I lived in Asheville, North Carolina—just over the mountain from Johnson City where they were waiting in a hotel. I felt dread as I drove the miles over the winding, twisting road that led me to my son. When I finally pulled into the hotel, I could see Betty waiting for me and I followed her into the room to where Jeff was waiting. As soon as I saw his white face, I knew that something bad had happened.

"Jeff told me how he had been driving around with his friend, Donald Strouth, who was also known as Chief. Chief had instructed Jeff to pull over in front of a used clothing store, saying he was going to rob it. Jeff thought he was joking and waited inside the car, never dreaming that Chief would actually go inside and hold it up. When Chief came out with blood on his jeans, Jeff knew that something had happened. It wasn't until hours later that Jeff found out on the news Chief had killed the elderly shopkeeper and stolen $200.

"All Jeff could think of was to get away from Chief, so he called me to come and get him and Betty. He refused to take any of the robbery money that Chief offered him. He wanted nothing to do with the crime.

"I moved Jeff and Betty to Greenville, South Carolina, until I could decide what to do about it. I knew hiding them was wrong, but I was afraid of Jeff's being put in jail. I would have to think of some other way to handle things. After finding them an apartment and seeing that both of them had jobs, I went back home to think about all that had happened.

"About a week later five detectives came to the Holiday Inn where I was a cocktail waitress. There, they questioned me for six hours in the back room, sometimes shouting loudly at me to tell them where my son was hiding. Detective Keesling was a tall, hard-looking man who told me that if the police should find Jeff, they would shoot to kill. He assured me that they only wanted him to come in and be tried as an accessory to a robbery. They had Chief in custody and knew that he alone had killed Mr. Keegan.

I refused to reveal where Jeff and Betty were, but I said I would tell Jeff what they had said and would let them know if he wanted to turn himself in.

"As I left the motel that night, my knees were buckling and I was afraid I would not make it to the car. Tears blinded my vision; I could barely see the road as I drove. As I screeched to a halt in front of the house, I screamed to my husband, Nelson. I began telling him what had happened, crying all the time and hardly taking a breath. He assured me that the police were right, that Jeff should come in and take his punishment—but there was something about the way the detectives had treated me that made me leery. I just had a feeling that something wasn't quite right. I wanted to trust Nelson and the police, but I just couldn't.

"I called Jeff the next day to tell him what had happened. He said he wanted to come in for he was not guilty. Even though he had taken none of the money from the robbery and had stayed in the car, he was willing to come in and face the charges.

"To our horror, when Jeff turned himself in, he was charged with first-degree murder. Fear overwhelmed me; my mouth went dry as I asked the detective why he was charging Jeff with murder. I started crying and re-minded him what he had told me, that Jeff would be charged as an accessory to a robbery. Detective Keesling told me that the charge would be changed during the trial. Jeff gave a statement, without an attorney present, that he had been present with Chief and had waited in the car.

"Jeff was taken to the jail in Blountville, Tennessee, not far from Kings-port. I went there to find an attorney who had handled a capital case before. Each attorney I went to told me he would need $100,000 for representing Jeff. The fact that Jeff had given a statement without an attorney present was going to make it hard for a lawyer to represent him. An attorney would never have let Jeff say that he was at the scene. The police had no other evidence linking Jeff to the crime.

"As I drove home that night, I wondered how I was going to raise the kind of money that was needed to ensure Jeff a fair trial. I felt as if I hadn't slept in a month, and all the news I had heard only made matters worse. We had a new home but had very little equity, so I knew that selling it would not bring enough money. I would have to borrow it somehow. My husband Nelson was home, and I told him what I had found out about the cost of a good attorney. He told me that Jeff would be given a court-appointed one and that was good enough. He didn't seem worried, and I started yelling at him that he didn't love Jeff. 'I will raise the money with or without you!' I shouted, running to my room.

"Betty was living with my three younger children and me. She was ex-pecting a baby in August. I had found out that I was also pregnant and didn't know where it would all end. How would we cope? The whole world was crashing down on top of me and I didn't know where to turn for comfort.

"In the weeks that followed, I worked two jobs to raise the money to find legal counsel. In the meantime, Jeff was appointed James Beeler from Kingsport as his attorney. He had never handled a capital case before, and he looked worried as he explained what was going to happen. He said Jeff's statement would be used against him and that he should never have been allowed to give one. All I knew of the legal system was from watching Perry Mason on television, where the bad guy always got caught and the innocent one was set free.

"Mr. Beeler said the state was going for the death sentence for Chief and Jeff. I felt faint and had to blink back the tears. This was a nightmare I was having and soon I would wake up to normal day-to-day living. But this nightmare went on and on. I knew I could not afford a good defense attorney, so I decided to find witnesses who might clear Jeff.

"Betty and I went to Kingsport to the scene of the crime. I began to question the people in the stores directly across the street from where Jeff had waited in the car. Suddenly, a policeman came over and told us to leave town. I tried to tell him that I was only trying to find someone who could testify that my son had waited inside the car that day, but again he yelled at us to leave town and not return.

"Instead of leaving town, we went to the hotel and I called the local television station. I told them what had happened and they sent a television crew out to interview me. I told them I needed to find someone who may have seen Jeff sitting in the car that morning. I gave them a picture of Jeff which they flashed on the screen as I talked into the camera. That night we saw it on the six o'clock news. It was supposed to run again at ten o'clock, but I got a telephone call from a man at the television station. He said he was sorry, but so many people had called in and said they did not want the mother of a murderer to be pleading for her son that they would not run it again. The people of this town had already tried my son and found him guilty before he even came to trial.

"The next morning we drove back to Asheville. I was discouraged and could do nothing but cry. How could I save Jeff when they all thought him guilty? My pregnancy was making me sick all the time, and I had to take care of the other children. Nelson was always there, but I could not talk to him about my feelings. He just said that everything was going to be all right. I heard that phrase over and over until I was ready to scream.

"Chief's trial was held in Kingsport, and they needed Betty to testify against him. The first to testify against Chief was his girlfriend, Barbara Davis. She told how Chief had come to her place of work that day in a car. She asked him how he would afford the car since she knew he hadn't had any money that morning. He told her he had robbed a shopkeeper and slit his throat.

"I felt sick listening to her testimony, but also glad that the jury was hearing how Chief alone had committed the murder. It never dawned on me that Jeff would have a different jury and they would not hear all this evidence. Little did we know that the prosecution had planned it this way. By trying them separately, Jeff's jurors would not hear all the evidence. Had they been tried together, Jeff would not have gotten the death sentence. They wanted to make an example of him.

"Barbara also testified that Chief called her to pick him up when his car broke down. When she got there, he was still wearing the bloodstained jeans. Barbara told him to rip them up and bury them in the woods. She later took police to the spot where the jeans were buried, and they were used as evidence.

"While listening to the testimony, I saw Chief look back at me with a smirk on his face, and again I felt faint. I felt the evil coming from him and I shuddered. Jeff had been so naïve to befriend this boy—but he had told me that Chief wasn't bad, he just didn't have a family who loved him.

"The next to take the stand was Jeff McMahan, a friend of Chief's who lived in High Point. He testified that Chief had called him the day of the murder and asked him to meet him at a convenience store. When McMahan arrived, he saw blood on Chief's jeans, and Chief confessed that he had killed an old man in a robbery. He said his partner had frozen up on him and waited in the car.

"I was beginning to feel better now that I heard McMahan's testimony. Surely they could not give Jeff the death sentence when so many people had told how Chief alone did the crime.

"The next to testify was Betty. She told how Chief and Jeff had picked her up that day and she had asked Chief how he had gotten blood on his hands and jeans. He told her that he had slit a man's throat.

"The used car salesman also testified that it was Chief who paid $200 cash for the used car.

"That night at our hotel, Betty brought McMahan in and I asked him if he would testify at Jeff's trial. He said the state was paying his week's wages and his hotel room. I told him that I would do the same if he would just testify at Jeff's trial about what Chief had told him. Offering him money would be one of the many mistakes I was to make.

"It didn't take the jurors long to come back with the guilty verdict and the death sentence. Chief didn't say anything, just looked back at his mother in the courtroom. I looked up and saw Detective Keesling looking at me with a self-satisfied grin and I had a sinking feeling. Suddenly I just knew they were going to do the same to Jeff. I felt stifled; the walls were closing in on me. I had to leave the courtroom and run outside for some air.

"I decided there was no way I could raise the kind of money I needed to hire a good attorney. I was desperate and time was running out. The jail they were holding Jeff in was a small place that only had two guards there during visiting hours on Sundays. I thought that the only way to save his life was to break him out of jail. When I told Nelson what I was planning to do, he looked at me as if I had lost my mind. There were times when I wondered if I had.

"'You're crazy,' he yelled. 'You're going to be sitting up there with Jeff. You can't get away with something so ridiculous. What if someone gets hurt?'

"I assured him that we were not going to use bullets in the gun. I had a small .22 pistol that I carried in the glove compartment of my car when I traveled. Sometimes I would go 1,000 miles to New Hampshire to visit relatives. Only the children and I would go, so I felt comfortable knowing that I could scare off anyone if my car broke down. I had never bought bullets for the gun as I was afraid one of the children would accidently set it off.

"I know now that I was bordering on insanity. Fear was driving me to do things no sane person would contemplate. At the time, though, it seemed the only answer. Nelson told me that he would not help in my crazy plan. I figured I would need three other men to hold the guards in the jail until Jeff and I had left. But how was I going to find someone to help me?

"Betty and I went to the roughest bar in Asheville. We were scared to death just seeing all the hard-looking people inside. We sat down, and a couple of Hispanic-looking men came over to the table. They didn't speak English well, but it was evident they were trying to make a pass. I asked the one sitting closest to me if he wanted to make some money. I had saved $3,000, and I figured that would be enough. He said sure, but when I said I needed some help in a jailbreak, he looked at me as if I were crazy. Together they got up laughing and yelling at the others in the bar what I had asked him. This wasn't going well. Betty and I quickly walked to the door and all but ran to the car.

"How do you go about finding someone to help? I wondered. I was beyond all reason now, and even my family was trying to talk me out of my plan. No one, I vowed, was going to kill my son while I was alive. I did find someone who said he would help me, but instead he went to the police with my plans. When we visited the jail the following Sunday, there were guards and police everywhere. We had noticed a state police car following us from the North Carolina border all the way to Blountville, but didn't know what was going on. When we went inside the jail for our visit, there was a huge female guard. She could have been a lady wrestler, and I noticed that she just kept staring at me. I was beginning to feel nervous. I knew something was going on. The atmosphere was too quiet, not the way it usually was. When we left the jail, we noticed that the police car was again following us back to the North Carolina border. It wasn't until we saw the newspaper the next day that we knew what had happened.

"'Deputies head off planned jailbreak,' I read. The article said that ten extra deputies had spent seven hours stationed around the jail. They had increased security because someone had tipped them off about a jailbreak that was to occur during the visiting hours. They said that Jeff Dicks was the center of the attempt and as of yet no arrests had been made.

"They moved Jeff to Brushy Mountain Prison, where security was tighter and not many people had escaped. Now I knew that the only way Jeff had of winning was to hire a competent attorney. It seemed everything was going from bad to worse, but I had to keep trying. I had to hold up and stay strong.

"I put my house up for sale, though I knew it wouldn't bring enough money. Day after day I thought of ways to get money, and finally I decided to write fraudulent checks. I would buy merchandise and sell it all at the flea market. It seemed to be the only answer. I just could not think of a legal way to raise the kind of money needed to defend Jeff. It was wrong to put such a high price on representation, and I cursed myself for not being wealthy.

"I went to another city and opened a checking account under a different name. I knew what I was doing was wrong, but at the time I didn't care what happened to me, if I could only get the money Jeff needed. Next I got a driver's license using a phony birth certificate and waited for the checks to come in.

"In the first store I went to, I placed the items on the counter. My mouth went dry, and I was shaking as I wrote the check. I just knew that everyone was watching me and that I would be caught at any minute. The sales clerk just smiled and gave me the bag. Quickly I ran outside, my heart pounding in my chest. I had made it. But at the next store the clerk questioned me more closely. He wanted to see more identification. I told him that I didn't have any on me, and that I would come back later, but he called the manager over. I didn't wait, but ran out of the store and sat in the car for five minutes until my breathing was normal again. For weeks I went from state to state opening bank accounts and buying merchandise.

"Back home again I felt safe, but I was getting weary. All the traveling back and forth was beginning to have its effect on me. I was tired and had lost weight even though I was five months pregnant. I started crying over everything and just didn't know what to do. Nelson tried to help me, but I pushed him away. He didn't understand my feelings. I loved Jeff and knew he was going through hell in prison. I had found out from a guard that another guard had thrown boiling water on him as he sat helpless in the cell. Another guard, when taking Jeff to the hospital, put a pistol to his head and begged him to make just one move so he could save the taxpayers the expense of a trial. I felt helpless and didn't know what to do or where to turn.

"The days we went up to visit Jeff were the hardest. He had gotten so thin that he looked like a skeleton. His eyes were dull and sunken in his face. It just tore me up to see him like that. We could not hug or kiss, but had to talk through a small hole in the door. In order to hear, you had to put your ear to the hole and listen, then look up to talk again. I couldn't say anything, just cry. Hard as I tried to hold myself together in front of Jeff, I couldn't do it. My heart was breaking, and I couldn't control my emotions. I wanted to kick the door down and take him away with me. Each visit he looked at me worriedly and said he was doing fine. I knew he was only saying that to ease my mind; he was being mistreated, and I was unable to help my son. I prayed to God to please spare his life; he was a good boy, he had just been in the wrong place at the wrong time.

"My oldest daughter, Tina, was working and she would give me all her money to help Jeff. She pleaded with me not to do anything else against the law. She was afraid that she would lose me too, and she could not bear that. I knew the pain I was causing my other children, but I was helpless to stop. I had one thing on my mind, and that was to save Jeff, no matter what I had to do. I explained to the kids that what I was doing was wrong, and I knew sooner or later I would have to pay for my crimes. Deep within me, I felt it would be worth it to be able to hire an experienced attorney for Jeff's defense. That's all I could think of—ways to get money. I couldn't eat or sleep, and it became an obsession to me.

"My grandmother lived in Massachusetts and I knew she had a Visa card. She had good credit and a high limit. I decided to travel the thousand miles and steal it from her to buy more merchandise. I knew she would not have to pay the charges once she reported it stolen.

"I visited with my grandmother for two days and had her Visa card in my wallet when it was time to leave. I felt guilty, but again I rationalized it by saying she would not have to pay the money back. I would have to face the guilt once it was known I had stolen the card. I wondered if there wasn't another way, but if there was, I couldn't think of it. I left Nana's that day feeling terrible, physically and mentally, yet determined to get on with the buying of merchandise.

"I hadn't gone far when I started bleeding. I checked into a hospital and lost the baby that night. Nelson flew in to be with me, and I signed myself out the next day. I had to start buying again. Time was running out.

"Barely able to stand, I went to the first store and used the card. My knees kept buckling under me but I had to go on. All the way to Asheville, I stopped at store after store.

"Betty had a baby girl, whom they named Shirley Maria, after me. We called her Maria to avoid confusion. She was a beautiful little girl and as I held her, I thought of the child I had lost. Pain filled me and I blinked back the tears and cuddled her close.

"The warden gave us permission to bring Maria to the prison for one hour. We would visit in a room with a guard present. At least we could give Jeff a hug and kiss. They also said we could bring in a camera and take some pictures of them together. I watched as Jeff very tenderly held his daughter. I saw the love and pride in his face and I knew the feelings he was having. He would want to protect his child, just like I was trying to protect him. When we left, I gave him a big hug and thought my heart would break as I felt his bony body close to mine. He was suffering, and I couldn't do anything for him. I would have gladly taken his place if I could have.

"My family kept telling me to let the justice system work, that I was going to get myself in so deep that I would be in prison along with Jeff. But nothing they said could penetrate my mind. All I could see was the state trying to murder my child. I loved him and I would die before I would let anyone kill him.

"My unlawful pursuits finally caught up with me in a small town in North Carolina. The clerk suddenly said she had to call the card in. I knew they didn't call the cards in if the amount was under $50, so I knew she suspected something. I told her never mind, that I didn't want the merchandise, but she was already on the phone. I ran out of the mall. Just as I was getting to my car, I saw the security car come flying around the corner and stop in front of the store. That marked the end of the credit card buying.

"With the U-Haul full of merchandise, I went to Florida each weekend to the flea market, then came back to visit Jeff on visiting day. Life was a roller coaster with no end in sight until I was able to hire an attorney in Asheville. His name was Larry Smith, and after telling him the facts, he assured me that Jeff would get probation. I told him how I was getting the money and said I would send him a money order every weekend from Florida.

"It was at this time that Betty decided to give the baby up for adoption. She felt she was too young to raise the child and didn't want the responsibility. I told her I would adopt Maria. I had the attorney draw up the papers and she signed them.

"Larry had given me hope which I clung to desperately. Mr. Beeler, the court-appointed attorney, was hesitant to tell me that Jeff would only get probation. He believed that Jeff would get time, a lot of it, but would not comment further. I felt uneasy and the fear was still there as much as I tried to push it aside. The trial was scheduled for February 5, 1979.

"Larry explained that anyone testifying at a trial would have to sit outside the courtroom. Since I was going to take the stand, I would not be allowed in. The jurors were finally picked, but all those who said they were against the death sentence were excluded. I felt weak and scared and knew Jeff was in for a big fight. I asked Larry where McMahan and Jeff's manager at work were; I had given him the telephone numbers so he could call them as witnesses. He told me he had everything under control and not to worry.

"The prosecution brought in Chief's bloodstained jeans and tried to make the jurors believe Jeff had worn them. After questioning from Larry Smith, they conceded the pants were the ones Chief had worn. They said Jeff was not working and needed the money from the robbery. Larry never called Mr. Clayton, Jeff's supervisor at Fuller Brush, to disprove it.

"Barbara Davis was called to the stand, and with the jurors out of the courtroom, the judge told her she could not tell anything Chief said to her about the crime. It was called hearsay evidence and was not admissible. She could not tell the jurors how Chief had said he slit the man's throat, or that he had spent all the money on a used car.

"I was getting tired of sitting outside and hearing about the testimony from family members. I asked Larry when he was going to call me to the stand. 'I decided not to call you,' he said. 'I think you would fall apart and that would look bad for Jeff.'

"Larry didn't call on Betty and didn't put on much of a defense. The jurors had not heard half of the evidence. Mr. Beeler said he would have called on McMahan and the Fuller Brush manager but he was not lead counsel so had to go along with whatever Larry said. I was really worried now that the trial was over and it was time for the closing arguments. We would be allowed in the courtroom for that part of the trial, and I sat down with my family.

"The prosecution began by saying that Jeff and Chief had both gone inside the store that day and slit Mr. Keegan's throat. I jumped up in my seat and began yelling it was not true. I wanted the jurors to know that Jeff had not gone inside with Chief that day. On and on I went. Through a fog, I could hear the judge rapping his gavel and telling the sheriff to put me in jail.

"I was put in a room with two other girls. From my cell I could see the room where the jurors were deliberating. I could hear their laughter and felt rage surge through my body. My son's life was at stake and it was as if they were laughing about it. The hours ticked by as I sat by the window watching, and waiting.

"I heard footsteps coming to the room and my heart stood still. It was Mr. Beeler, and I walked slowly over to where he stood patiently waiting for me. I couldn't read his face, but when he said, 'I'm sorry,' I screamed. Jeff had been found guilty of murder. I covered my ears and backed away from the door crying. The girls put their arms around me, but I couldn't be comforted. The next part of the trial was to decide if Jeff was to get life imprisonment or the death sentence. Again I waited by the window watching the jury room. I wanted to plead with these 12 people to have mercy for my child. Where was God? I wondered. How could he let this happen?

"Suddenly the back door of the courthouse opened and I could see my daughter Tina coming slowly out in the yard, her bent bent low, her long brown hair covering her face. I knew in that instant the jurors had given Jeff the death sentence. Time seemed to stop, and I couldn't catch my breath; darkness was coming over me.

"'No!' I screamed over and over. 'You can't do that to my son. He's innocent! You can't send him to die. Oh God, no!' The screams went on and on and I held on the bars. The room was spinning around and around. I could hear my mother's voice yelling up at me to hold on. She was begging me to stop, saying we would fight it, but I had no mind left and the screams continued.

"The door opened and my mother and a nurse came in. She gave me a shot and then I went off into darkness. The next morning, the guard came up and told me I could leave if I promised to be quiet. I agreed and was led down to the sheriff's office. There my family was waiting and we were told to leave Tennessee and not return.

"A police car escorted us to the city line and one of the officers came over to the car. He told me that he couldn't believe Jeff had gotten the death sentence. He had been in the courtroom and heard all the testimony. He said he was sorry, but he had a job to do.

"I knew I would have to leave North Carolina with my two youngest children, Trevor and Maria. The state marshall had come during Jeff's trial to question me about the checks and the credit card. I was supposed to come to his office as soon as I came back to Asheville. Jeff had been taken to Nashville, where death row was located, and I would not be able to see him.

"Nelson was going back to New York and would take our daughter Laurie with him. She was 16 years old now and did not want to go on the run. Because of all the turmoil we had filed for divorce and it was almost final, but Nelson told me to call if I ever needed anything.

"I kissed my parents and daughters goodbye. We were all crying and I said I would get in touch with them as soon as I was settled. Now I had lost Jeff and also my family. I was alone and thinking of just ending it all. I couldn't do that, my mind kept telling me. I had Trevor and Maria and the rest of the family to think of. They all loved me and I couldn't do that to them.

"Texas was the first place that seemed friendly enough, and I found a trailer for us to live in. Calling my family before the police had the phones tapped, I gave them my phone number so they could call me from the outside pay phones. I knew it wouldn't be long before the warrants would be out for my arrest.

"I was only there for a month when I broke all the bones in my ankle. I was taken to the hospital where I had surgery to repair the damage. I had to stay for two weeks. The surgery was painful but somehow I welcomed the pain. It took my mind off Jeff. My mother told me he was doing all right and they had driven the 300 miles to see him. The FBI had been to question Jeff about my disappearance.

"For the next year I was in a cast and a wheelchair. Trevor took care of Maria and did a lot of the cooking. I couldn't seem to get myself together and constantly wondered how Jeff was doing. I had gotten cassette tapes from him, sent by my mother in another state. I received a Mother's Day card from him, and I felt the tears starting as I read the words he wrote: "Mom, Tho I don't say it very often, I want to say I love you. I'm very lucky to have such a special mother. I wouldn't trade you for my freedom. Thank you for always being there for me. I've never been good at showing my feelings, but always know that I love you mom and you make me proud."

"Finally, I called my mother and asked her to tell the FBI that I would turn myself in if they would guarantee that I could visit Jeff one time before they sentenced me. My daughters, Tina and Laurie, didn't want me to come in. They had paid back the credit card charges but were afraid I would spend years in prison. I knew I would have to face up to the crimes I had committed, and I could not go on any longer without my family. I had to see Jeff again, no matter what price I had to pay.

"The FBI agreed I could go to Tennessee and see Jeff if I came in. I packed up Trevor and Maria, and we came back to North Carolina. I was taken to the courthouse, and after I had waited a while, the officer came to talk to me. He said if I pleaded guilty, the judge would give me a fine and a year's probation. I readily agreed to this and was released.

"The first time I saw Jeff was just great. I couldn't hold back the tears as I held him. He hadn't known that I was turning myself in because I didn't want to worry him. He looked down at me and said he loved me. How I loved this man-child of mine. He held his daughter and she didn't appear to be afraid of him.

"For the next year, I traveled back and forth every weekend to visit Jeff. The trip took six hours each way and was tiring and expensive, so I decided to move to Nashville to be near him. I found a small trailer and we moved in. This way we could visit twice a week with Jeff and get him out of his cell.

"I wrote to F. Lee Bailey and all the famous attorneys I could find. I was trying to find one that could find a mistake in the trial and have his sentence overturned. Larry Smith was no longer our attorney. Since the trial, he had been disbarred for perjury. I found Bart Durham of Nashville. He took us back to the postconviction hearing. The same judge and prosecution were there. Bart tried to convince the judge that Smith, as lead attorney, did not provide adequate counsel. I had to go on the stand and apologize to the judge for my outburst in the previous trial. I didn't want to apologize because I felt the judge knew Jeff was innocent. He was the same judge as had been on Chief's trial.

"Mr. Beeler said he disagreed with Smith's approach and defense of Jeff because he did not subpoena witnesses that we have given him, and because he had put Jeff on the stand unprepared. He said Larry had not discussed a strategy and that he had not been made party to the case preparation. He said Smith would not return his calls about the case and that friction had developed between them during the trial.

"Others testifying were state's witnesses who said they were not interviewed by defense lawyers. Smith responded to those allegations by saying that no witnesses would talk to him and that he could not find any beneficial witnesses. Larry said I had offered money to McMahan to change his testimony. McMahan had told Mr. Beeler the same thing before I even met him, so he couldn't change it. I never wanted him to change his testimony, just come to Jeff's trial and testify. I felt like slapping Smith in the face as he stood on the stand and said that. I had offered to pay McMahan's way over and the hotel room and food. He could not afford to come over otherwise, and I thought his testimony was important. I didn't want him to change anything he had already testified to.

"McMahan got on the stand and told how he had talked to me. He said I had offered him money to come and testify for Jeff the way the state had. 'I can only tell you what Chief said down at the bridge. And he said his partner froze up in the car. I don't give a damn whether she sends me the money or not. When he said froze up, that means the guy stayed in the car,' he said.

"Back in Nashville we waited for the outcome of the hearing. It came back upheld. The judge would not agree that Jeff should have a new trial. Bart said to keep my spirits up, that the fight was not over. He assured me that Jeff would get a new trial in the federal level. I wanted to believe him with all my heart, but my head told me different.

"The years went on and Maria was starting school. She had grown up suddenly, and I felt a pang as she went off to her first day of school. We took pictures so Jeff could see things she was doing. He wanted to participate in her life as much as possible. She loved playing with him when she visited the prison, often making him carry her piggyback around the small room in which we had our visits. The judge and district attorney took themselves off the case, but they are still on Strouth's case. This is very unusual and it only means one thing to me. They feel guilty knowing they sent an innocent man to death row."

Wrongful Convictions

Timothy Hennis

In North Carolina in 1986, Timothy Hennis was sentenced to die in the electric chair for the murder of a woman and two of her daughters. His family wept as they heard the verdict. The jury returned the death sentence after three hours of deliberation.

The victims were found in their home on May 12, 1985, with stab wounds and cut throats. Hennis claimed he was innocent of the crime and was depressed that he was not believed. He told investigators that he had met the slain woman when he answered an advertisement seeking a home for the family's pet English setter.

Assistant District Attorney William Van Story IV said he didn't believe legal errors had been committed during the trial that could lead to a reversal on appeal. He said it would be difficult to determine what factors in the circumstantial case led the jurors to think him guilty. He said the jury obviously believed the witness, Patrick Cone, who said he saw Hennis walking out of the driveway around 3:30 that day. He said the jury also believed Lucille Cook, who said Hennis looked like a man she saw using an automatic teller machine on May 11, when Mrs. Eastburn's bank card was used to withdraw $150.

For three years Hennis sat on death row until the Supreme Court ordered a new trial because the state's use of victims' photographs may have inflamed the jury.

Charlotte Kirby said she couldn't stand it anymore. She had been a newspaper carrier and had seen a man walking across the yard the day of the murder. She later saw this man at a fast-food restaurant when she had finished delivering the papers. She said she saw a light-colored van near the Eastburns' driveway. She told the jury how the man she had seen was about 5'7" with a medium build and wearing a toboggan hat and carrying a green laundry bag over his shoulder.

"I thought if I didn't say anything, Mr. Hennis would spend some time in jail, and the man would come forward," she said. She told them that when Hennis's picture was put in the paper after his arrest, it did not look like the man she had seen. A friend urged her to come forward and tell the truth about what she had seen. She said she hadn't because about that time she had begun getting threatening calls.

A key prosecution witness testified earlier in the trial that he saw the defendant, dressed in a Member's Only jacket and a toboggan hat, with a bag over his shoulder, walking down the driveway at around 3:30 that afternoon.

It took the jury two hours before declaring Hennis not guilty and he walked out of the Hanover County Courthouse a free man. As the jury read the verdict, members of Hennis's family burst into tears and closed their eyes. Hennis said he planned to report to Fort Bragg and expected to go to Fort Knox, Kentucky, to clear up his Army status.

Some of the jurors said they had a reasonable doubt and could not convict Hennis on the evidence that was presented. The state's evidence just didn't convict him. The jury deliberated in the case while attorneys continued with a hearing on a defense motion to dismiss the case based on a defense allegation that the prosecution withheld documents and witnesses that could have aided Hennis. That hearing was halted when the jury announced it had reached a verdict. Defense attorneys said prosecutors ignored trial rules by failing to tell the defense about witnesses and documents that could have aided his defense. The defense attorneys focused much of their argument on John Andrew Raupach, who was interviewed by a prosecutor and three investigators while Hennis was on trial.

Hennis's attorneys said eyewitnesses in the case could have mistaken Hennis for Raupach. They said that under rules of discovery, prosecutors should have told them about Raupach. Van Story, the assistant district attorney, testified that he was not obligated to tell the defense because Raupach was not considered a suspect.

After the second trial, jurors said that Raupach's presence in the Eastburn neighborhood caused them to doubt that Hennis was the man seen on the night of the slayings. The defense motion stated prosecutors did not provide the defense with other information potentially helpful to Hennis in time for effective use, including the following: photographs of a shoeprint found in the investigation could not determine the shoe size; details of head and pubic hairs not belonging to Hennis or any member of the Eastburn family, that such hairs were found in the Eastburn house; a Fort Bragg Crime Prevention Checklist that strongly supported the defendant's alibi; the name Ilsa Peabody, an Eastburn neighbor who testified that she saw Hennis at the Eastburn house a day before the murders; and details about an Eastburn neighbor rumored to have argued with Mrs. Eastburn in front of the Winn-Dixie store.

Investigators testified they interviewed Raupach and he told them he often walked home from his job. Raupach told them he often wore corduroy pants at work and frequently wore a dark Members Only jacket and a beret and often carried a knapsack over his shoulder. He told officers he had a collection of knives and read survival books and the mercenary magazine *Soldier of Fortune.*

It was noted that bloody corduroy-like impressions were found on bed-clothes in Mrs. Eastburn's bedroom. Raupach and Hennis also looked alike in height, weight, and hair color. Van Story said Raupach offered nothing that offset evidence of Hennis's guilt or exonerated Hennis. He said Raupach had an alibi for the times Mrs. Eastburn's stolen bank card was used.

Detective Watts testified that on the night before Van Story interviewed Raupach, the youth gave authorities his jacket and knapsack. Watts said he put them in the trunk of his car without testing them for a possible connection to the murders. He also said he made no report of having the items in his possession.

Jurors said reasonable doubt led them to acquit Timothy Baily Hennis on the murder and rape charges. "I don't feel like he did it," said juror Joseph Corbett. "I think he got a fair trial, and he got what he deserved."

Mrs. McDowell, another juror, said, "We kept coming back to the idea that Hennis didn't have to prove his innocence; the state had to prove his guilt, and the state couldn't prove his guilt. They could never put him inside the Eastburn house on the night of the slayings."

The jurors all sympathized with Gary Eastburn, the husband and father of the victims. "I cried with him, and I hope to God the murderer is found and punished for what he did to the family," Mrs. McDowell said. "But I hope they get the right man, and I don't think Hennis is the right man."

Randall Dale Adams

It was Thanksgiving weekend in 1976 when a police officer was gunned down and a manhunt ensued. Randall Dale Adams was convicted of the murder and sent to death row. His ordeal began when 16-year-old David Harris offered him a ride after Randall's car broke down.

They spent the day together, and Adams claims that Harris dropped him off at his motel room around 10 P.M. Harris testified that they left a drive-in around midnight with Adams driving the car. He said police officer Robert Wood pulled their car over and Adams pulled out a gun and fired five shots into the officer. It was later learned that Harris had previously stolen the weapon.

Police questioned Harris when friends of his said he had been talking about killing a police officer. Still the police believed him when he said Adams did the killing. It only took six months before Adams was tried and convicted of the murder and sentenced to die in Texas.

It wasn't until 1985 that Errol Morris came to Texas to do a documentary about a psychiatrist who testified in death penalty cases, and stumbled across Adams's story.

In its zeal to help Morris, the Dallas district attorney's office turned over the records from Adams's trial. What he found in the prosecutor's files shocked him. The slain officer's partner had told police at first that it was too dark and the windows were too dirty to see who had committed the murder. Then she testified that the killer had bushy hair like Adams. The prosecution argued that the defense could not cross-examine her because she was traveling. She was in fact staying at a motel in Dallas. She finally revealed to Morris that she had failed to pick Adams out of a lineup.

Morris decided that he would not do a story on Dr. James Grigson, but would instead do a documentary on Randall Adams in *The Thin Blue Line*. This has won two major film awards and helped Adams to win his freedom.

All the evidence pointed to Harris. Both the car and the pistol had been stolen by Harris, and he had been in trouble before. Still, the prosecution bought his story. Adams's attorney, Randy Schaffer, contends that Harris supplied two things the prosecution wanted: an eyewitness (Harris) and someone to execute (Adams). Harris was too young for the death penalty.

Adams got a major break when Schaffer took his case in 1982 for expenses only. Then Morris began filming in 1985. The investigating officers sat before him in their best suits, preening for the camera, as did two prosecution witnesses whose stories fell apart. Most chilling of all, Harris all but confesses, saying to Morris, "I'm the one who knows" Adams is innocent.

On March 1, an appellate court unanimously threw out Adams's conviction, finding that the state was guilty of suppressing evidence favorable to Adams, deceiving the trial court and knowingly using perjured testimony.

Adams was released and flown home to Ohio where his mother and family and friends were gathered. The next day his sister threw a party. Adams, now 40, seems to have made his peace with his jailers, knowing that to pursue revenge could poison his future happiness. He has learned to think the worst and hope for the least.

Doug Mulder, the former Dallas prosecutor who wronged him, is shielded by law from suits by convicts.

But cases like Adams's leave a residue of uneasiness; if the court had not reversed the death sentence, and if a filmmaker had not stumbled onto suppressed evidence in locked and forgotten files, Adams would have been dead long ago.

James Richardson

For 21 years James Richardson was in prison. He had been convicted of killing his seven children in 1967. The six girls and one boy began convulsing not long after eating lunch at their home in Arcadia, Florida. By the next morning, all of them were dead, poisoned by a potent insecticide.

The prosecution contended that Richardson, an illiterate farm worker, had killed his family to collect insurance. In 1989 his lawyers petitioned the court to overturn the conviction by claiming that prosecutors knowingly used perjured testimony and withheld evidence. A special investigation followed, and Governor Martinez appointed a judge to decide if Richardson should be released.

The documents that Richardson's attorneys relied on paint a damaging picture of the original proceedings. For one thing, an insurance agent had explained to investigators that the children were not insured. The prosecution had evidence that completely refuted an insurance motive. The statements were never furnished to the defense.

Who did poison the children if Richardson did not? Some believe it was the babysitter who served the children lunch that day. Betsy Reese, who served time for shooting her husband, was believed to be angry at Richardson because he had introduced her husband to his cousin, and the two reportedly ran off together.

As this book goes to press, Reese, 67 and in the advanced stages of Alzheimer's disease, is no longer competent to stand trial. In 1989 two nursing home attendants said in affadavits that Reese had confessed to the crime when she was lucid.

Richardson believes he has made good use of his time in prison. He was sentenced to die, but that sentence was eventually overturned to 25 years. He learned to read and later got a GED. His wife lives in Jacksonville, and she has no photographs of her dead children."It's a terrible feeling knowing I could have died for something I didn't do, but then I tell myself that if I die, I would be going home to my children."

Joseph Green Brown

Joseph Brown confessed to a burglary he committed with an accomplice. The accomplice got even by accusing Brown of a murder in Florida. Brown was tried and sentenced to death. Eventually, experts declared that Brown's gun was not the murder weapon. The 11th Circuit Court of Appeals granted habeas corpus relief after the state conceded that the prosecution had deliberately withheld the fact that Brown's accuser had failed polygraph tests about his testimony, and eight months after the trial admitted he had lied. Brown, who came within hours of being executed and had been measured for his burial suit in 1985, was released after 13 years on death row.

Shortly after the suit had been measured, he was asked to order his last meal — anything he wanted. He rejected the offer as insulting. As he sweated out his time, there were scores of convicts throughout America's prison system who were doing time for crimes that were almost identical to the one for which he had been convicted.

Those who were truly dangerous among these criminals would, or should, never be released. Others, after serving long terms, would be released on parole, and scarcely a soul among them would be returned to prison for a subsequent crime.

Why hadn't Brown been permitted to join this favored majority? Why had he and a small fraction of other felons been singled out to die while vastly larger numbers of criminals paying penance for misdeeds virtually the same as his were allowed to work out their destiny?

The absence of answers, which emphasizes the blind inequity of the death penalty, is another major reason why its use is immoral and unacceptable. But in Brown's case, the questions were really academic because he was innocent.

The circuit court ordered a new trial. Before it could begin, the original witness admitted he had lied and the state, sensing it had no case, abandoned its prosecution. Brown was released, a free man, with his only possessions being the clothes on his back and his legal papers. Between the ages of 23 and 37, he had spent the rich marrow of his youth on death row.

This illuminates the most sordid defects of capital punishment. Brown's blackness and his poverty helped doom him. He was ruthlessly cheated; it was never his privilege to be granted, even for a phantom crime, the incarceration that is meted out to others and that carries the possibility of redemption. He would not have died a criminal but a victim whose innocence would have been as surely entombed as his body in its burial suit.

John Henry Knapp

John Henry Knapp was convicted in two separate trials of the arson murder of his two children. Only after a Federal court stayed Knapp's execution after his state appeal was new evidence discovered supporting Knapp's claim of innocence. Knapp sought a second round of review in state court and was given a new trial based on new scientific evidence, not available at the time of his original trials, to show that the fire was actually started by the children. The state dropped all charges, and the case was dismissed in 1987.

Henry Drake

Both Drake and a co-defendant, William Campbell, were convicted and sentenced to death for the murder of a barber shop owner in 1975. A volunteer lawyer who took Drake's appeal in 1979 discovered that Campbell, the sole witness against Drake, had recanted his testimony and admitted that he alone committed the murder. But Campbell's lawyer was bound by lawyer-client confidentiality. In 1985 the 11th Circuit Court of Appeals reversed Drake's sentence because of trial procedure errors. He was given a life sentence.

It was only in 1987, when Campbell died of natural causes, that his lawyer came forward with the exonerating information. The Georgia Board of Pardons and Paroles released Drake at Christmas 1987.

Zel Morris

Wife of Death Row Inmate

"I don't feel any different from any other married woman, with the exception that Tim does not share my bed. I met Tim while tending bar in Florida. I remember his sad, blue eyes the first time I saw him and that's what attracted me to him. I wanted to wrap him up in my arms and make him happy. We spent many days and nights together, talking and laughing and finally falling in love. We were the best of friends and we didn't know that we were really in love until Tim was arrested for this crime. We just thought we were best friends and it wasn't until he was snatched away did we know the feelings we had were love.

"Several police cars, county sheriffs, and other law enforcement officers surrounded the small trailer where we lived and took Tim down to the police station to question him about a murder committed in Tennessee and then released him. Several weeks later Tim was taken to Greenville to await trial for the murder. I went to Greenville and worked for three months and visited with Tim every day. Then I would go back to Florida and work for three months to keep the payments up on my mobile home. I just ran back and forth for a year until Tim went to trial. He was sentenced to death. I remember running from the courthouse, my heart breaking and tears streaming down my face. I kept thinking about what had happened and decided that I could not spend my life waiting for a man condemned to die.

"I moved back to Florida and tried to forget Tim, but it was useless. I loved him more than I ever thought possible and decided that right or wrong, I was going to be by his side.

"Once again I moved, this time to Nashville, where death row was located. I found a small apartment and found a job as a waitress near the prison. I was allowed to visit with Tim twice a week and that's all I lived for.

"It wasn't common knowledge that Tim was on death row but it wasn't anything I was ashamed of, to know that I was in love with someone in prison. I shared the fact that he was on death row with my closest friends.

"People assume that Tim is guilty just because he was convicted. They don't believe that the innocent can be found guilty and sentenced to die but it's been proven by a study by Hugo Bedau and Michael Radelet that 350 cases of wrongly convicted people were sent to death row. Half of the people I met felt sorry for me but didn't want to get too close, the other half came right out and asked me if they were going to fry him. This scares me, and it hurts that people can be so cruel. They're either scared of me or they act like I have something contagious, so most of my closest friends are those who also have a loved one on death row.

"We have to stick together until the rest of the world really can learn to accept the fact that we didn't do anything, we're human like everyone else. I think the death penalty is a lottery and Tim's number was picked. After a while we decided to get married. We ran into trouble because the state of Tennessee had never allowed a death row inmate to be married. For a year I had to fight the system and finally the warden gave permission for us to be married.

"Our wedding was on the front page of the local newspapers and some around the rest of the country. I got a lot of death threats, a lot of people being nosy who wanted to strike out and hurt. And it did. After a while a lot of it died down when people found out that it wasn't just something I had been going through, that I really loved Tim. There's still a lot of cruel people around, but I've found there are a lot of good people too. Those who have someone on the row are like family. We're all one and the same, and can share and relate to one another. We're victims just like the family of the person who was killed. The only difference is their loved one is dead and buried in the ground, and our loved one is one of the living dead.

"It's hard to make new friends because if you're honest enough to tell them where your husband is, they think you're scum. People come to my house and are amazed that I have electricity and an inside toilet. I feel I've become much stronger and I've learned that you have to fight for what you think is right.

"I think it has come to the point in society where you have to prove yourself innocent instead of the state proving you guilty. I spend the majority of my time waiting. Waiting to go to the prison, waiting to get in, and then when I leave, waiting until I can come back again. I think the biggest injustice is all the innocent people convicted of crimes they didn't do, being lumped with those who admit their guilt—then the state selects who will get the death sentence, and who will go free. There's nothing right with that starting from the jury, and now you cannot even sit on a jury if you do not believe in the death penalty. Then they are shipped out to a death row where they are caged like animals with nothing to look forward to, without a reason to live. That leaves us victims on the outside gasping for air just to breathe, to get alone without the people we love, and to fight for their lives.

"I think the most difficult thing I've had to deal with is the public in general. They need to be more educated about the death penalty. I find it a very lonely life if you're not surrounded by family and friends, and loneliness is a major thing I fight.

"I got a better job with the Coalition on Jails and Prisons and quit my job as a waitress. The men on death row would call me daily with problems which I did my best to help, or I would just listen to those who were lonely. I worked there for four years and during that time I learned just how unjust our justice system really is.

"I think what would improve the state and the community would be for people to get more involved. Not necessarily with the death row inmates, but with prisons in general. They don't think that it could happen in their families. If they would go and visit a prison, or just talk to an inmate's family, I feel that they would get a little insight on what we are going through and it would bring a better understanding among all of us.

"I have spoken out several times publicly against the death penalty and my feelings about it. About how we as family and friends are treated. It's real, real unfair. A lot of times we are mistreated by the public like we're the ones who committed the crimes. A lot of the times when we visit the people in prison that we love and care about, we're discriminated against by the very same people that are supposed to be there to protect rights.

"A lot of the guards are very nice, but there are others who shouldn't be working in the system because they let their personal feelings get in the way of how they do their job. I've never been personally harassed by the guards but have seen it done to many other people. We've been made to wait outside in rain and snow for as long as six hours just to get inside the prison itself. Then once inside, we may get an hour to visit.

"We're allowed to take three dollars in change for the snack machines we pass on the way to death row. It depends on the mood of the person in charge that day if we are allowed to take a soda or candy bar over with us.

"You're not allowed to have that much personal contact or touching with someone on the row. You can hold hands, but you're not allowed to pet or neck. I suppose that's for everyone's protection, but sometimes that's carried a little too far. The guards stand and watch you during the visit through a glass door and it's like visiting in a fish bowl.

"There was a time when we were allowed to occasionally share a meal with our loved one. I remember we used to be able to have a dinner four times a year with the death row inmates and families. The Prison Ministry would bring in hamburgers and french fries and we would all sit down and enjoy just having a meal with our husbands and sons and fathers. There was never any trouble but prison officials stopped that. Now we're lucky if we can sit down and share a cup of coffee together.

"The major gripe I have is the inmate cannot use the restroom during a visit. The visitor can use it but we have to terminate our visit if the inmate should have to use the bathroom. This to me is cruel and inhumane.

"It's hard to survive when you have a loved one on death row, especially if you are a woman alone. Now we have only one salary instead of two to live on. I've worked as many as three jobs in order to keep food on the table and a car to drive and a semidecent place to live.

"I believe the death penalty is wrong. I never did believe in it, but until this happened to Tim, I did believe that everyone who got the death penalty was guilty. That didn't make it right, but it did make me think about it less. I believed that our justice system was perfect, that it didn't convict innocent people. I found out the hard way and during the trial I learned that in reality the state didn't have to prove Tim's guilt but rather, we had to prove his innocence.

"The attorney appointed to represent Tim was inexperienced in capital cases. But without money, and lots of it, an experienced attorney was not available to him. Tim was expected to provide proof of innocence, beyond a reasonable doubt, to a jury composed of death penalty proponents.

"I also learned during trial that you don't have to be guilty beyond a reasonable doubt to be convicted, circumstantial evidence is enough to send you to death row. The state then has the lawful power and privilege to commit the very same crime for which you were unable to prove your innocence—premeditated murder. The state can and does kill people to show that killing is wrong.

"I married Tim because I love him. I married him for the same reason any woman marries another man. I don't feel any different from any other woman who is married. Why would I marry a man on death row? I've had this question asked of me many times before and the only thing I can say to you as a reader, is I'd rather have a day, a week, or a year with Tim, even under these conditions, than I would a lifetime with any other person.

"I always have to say that there is a possibility that he won't get out, but I know in my heart that he will come home. That's all I live for. We are very much in love and where he is I'll be, and where I'll be, he will be. The only thing separating us is the bars. We're just people, like everyone else, and we've got the same feelings."

Poem by Zel Morris

As I sit here alone, and think about olden time
I realize the truth . . . I'm a victim of crime. It's hard to remember
Just when it began, But life is so precious, I remember the end

A beautiful day, The sun shone bright. In our world of love
Everything was right. A dark cloud appeared, in a uniform of blue
A blurry time thereafter, 'Cause there was no more you.

There were no shots fired, no blood was shed. A jury of your peers
Just rendered you dead. A life condemned, a death warrant signed
The end of your freedom, the loss of my mind

I visit you weekly, we hold each other tight. And talk of times
When everything was right. It's a very sad story, but one that is true
We're victims of crime, both me and you.

We're poorer now than we were back then. But love still binds us, and
we know we'll win. A murder is committed, one person is dead
An eye for an eye, that's what they all said

The public cries out, revenge is their name. Legalized murder
is the name of the game. Kill him, kill him! Pay him his due
Give him the chair, let him die too.

The fact that you're innocent, is the part they don't hear
It's your premeditated murder and yet they don't shed a tear
The judges and juries, and witnesses too, weighed all the evidence, and
decided what to do.

A murder was committed, and someone must pay. Like a name in a lottery
It was your time and day. It's a very sad story, but one that is true
We're victims of crime, both me and you.

Sarah Easley

Mother of Executed Son

"I have never felt such pain as I did the night my son Jimmy Wingo died. I didn't think I would live through it, and I'm not sure that I wanted to, but somehow I found the strength through God. I just felt that I couldn't bear that kind of pain, but when Jimmy died, there was such a sweet spirit that came into the car. A friend and I were driving away from the prison and were on the way home after spending time with Jimmy. He hadn't wanted me to stay outside the prison until it was over; he wanted me to be home when it happened. The family members had to leave six hours before an execution in Louisiana so we couldn't stay at the prison with him.

"We would cry so hard we'd have to pull the car over to the side of the road and just sit there and cry and talk about Jimmy. I was hoping for a miracle, but I knew in my heart it wouldn't happen. I sincerely hope no other mother will have to go through that kind of pain again, and praise God maybe they won't. At ten minutes after twelve, the lady that was with me said that something was happening. I could feel the peace that surrounded us. I can't describe it, but the car was filled with peace, and we didn't shed any more tears that night. It's as if the Lord said to us, 'It's all right, Jimmy is home with me.' So that's how I handled it. I know that the Lord blessed me, He was there with me and I was never alone.

"The last day we went in at eight and spent the day until six that evening with Jimmy. Jimmy would talk to his children, telling them not to let this make them bitter. He was innocent but he told them that he would be with the Lord soon and away from all the pain. It was so hard to visit knowing this was the last time I would see my son alive and it took all I had not to break down. All too soon it was time to leave and we said our good-byes.

"I remember when Jimmy found out he was wanted for murder, he got his girlfriend and they hid out in the woods for twelve days. They had no food or water and were scared to death. I felt fear because I knew they were hunting him like an animal with guns and dogs. They had him surrounded but couldn't get him. Finally he just gave himself up and no one was hurt.

"I was terrified about the whole thing when I heard about it. Jimmy had been in jail on another charge when he decided to escape with Jimmy Glass, a friend of his. I had this terrible dread, like doom was impending on me. I had told Jimmy not to do anything rash when he called me and said he had to get to his girlfriend.

"When all this happened, my husband began acting funny and wouldn't come home or comfort me. Jimmy wasn't his son, and he blamed me for the trouble he was in now. He kept telling me over and over that they were going to kill Jimmy this time. I don't know if he realized how much he was hurting me with his cruel words. Jimmy was my son and I loved him. I didn't want to hear that he was going to be killed. I wanted to feel the comfort of my husband's arms around me. I wanted him to hold me and let me cry on his shoulder, but he didn't. I had to go through it all alone. It got so bad I was afraid to turn on the television or listen to the news, afraid of what I would hear.

"My Jimmy and Jimmy Glass just walked out of jail that day. Glass had tattoos on his arms and didn't have a shirt to cover them so my Jimmy gave him his shirt to wear. Jimmy was coming home to see about his girlfriend. She had been in trouble and Jimmy had called me and asked if I could bring her there to visit with him. I told him that I had no way to do that, so he said he would just leave, that he had to see her. When I hung up, I started to call the jail and tell the jailer not to let Jimmy out. They were trustees and could walk around at will.

"My husband told me to let him grow up and stop making his decisions for him. I thought, well, let it fall where it will. He was only in there for simple burglary. Since it was his first offense we expected him to get probation.

"My husband and I went up to his son's house as it was the 23rd of December so Jimmy couldn't get hold of me anymore. Once outside the jail, Jimmy started thumbing a ride. Glass went the other way. Jimmy walked for a long time before he could get a ride. He stood in the rain and waited for a car to come by. Then a car stopped, and Jimmy Glass was driving. My Jimmy knew the car was stolen but he got in anyway. Glass still had Jimmy's shirt on and there were traces of blood on it.

"They drove on to the house where the boys changed clothes because they were wet. Jimmy and his girlfriend went on to the motel to talk things over so they could decide what they were going to do and Glass went somewhere else. They were there when they heard on the news that Jimmy was wanted for murder of an elderly couple.

"Once in custody both boys were finally convicted and sentenced to die. I thought my heart would break. I knew my son wasn't capable of killing anyone and I prayed that God would save him, that he would somehow have Jimmy Glass tell the truth, that my Jimmy wasn't with him when he killed the couple.

"On Saturday, October 8, 1983, Jimmy wrote me a letter that almost broke my heart. I'll share a few parts of it with you.

My dearest Mother, I love you, Mom, more tonight than I ever knew before. I hope that you can understand all that I'm about to say. God showed me tonight how much He truly loved me. I want to ask you to forgive me for all the pain and sorrow that I have brought into your life through the years. I know that there's no way I can take back all the nights that you must have lain in tears, trying to figure out what you did or didn't do to keep me from showing you how much I loved you. I could never be close to you the way I should have been, and I really don't know why, for God in heaven knows that a more loving and caring mother never lived in this world like you. I can't remember telling you while I was growing up that I was proud of you for being the beautiful lady that you truly are. I never realized until tonight how foolish and blind I've been for so many years. I've never felt the sorrow and pain before that I live with tonight. I suppose the hardest thing for any of us to do is to admit that we were wrong and evil. God showed me what it means to suffer and love someone, for He revealed unto me the many times that I persecuted Him, and tore the heart and soul that I know He has. I felt like I died tonight inside, my heart felt as if it would explode and I couldn't bear it another minute. All I can do is say I'm sorry and ask that you forgive me, as I know God has, and I'll not make promises anymore that I can't keep. All I can do is hope and pray that I never cause anyone else to suffer the sorrow and pain that I felt this night, ever again. I love you, Mama, with all my heart, and I'm very proud of you. I'll close for now, God bless you and be with you all, as He is now with me. Be sweet, and take care, love always, Your son, Jimmy.

"The Lord let me know that Jimmy and I weren't alone. He was there with us and it was that faith that sustained me throughout this whole ordeal. My husband walked out about that time and didn't even try to contact me. He had nothing to do with Jimmy either. He didn't send money to help me out, didn't ask if we were eating all right; he just stayed gone.

"The first thing that Jimmy said to me when I was finally able to visit with him was, 'Mama, I didn't kill anyone.' The prison at Angola, Louisiana, was a six-hour drive and I just didn't have any way to get there. I already knew in my heart that Jimmy hadn't killed anyone and I asked him how was I going to prove that? Jimmy had a court-appointed attorney who sold him down the drain. He was friends with the DA and didn't put up a fight to save his life.

"It was so hard to raise the money to get to Angola to visit with Jimmy. It was so far we'd have to stay at a motel overnight and it would cost about one hundred dollars. For someone who just gets by, we couldn't raise the money very often so we didn't get to visit with Jimmy as much as I would have liked to do.

"James Allison would take me and the grandkids over to visit with

Jimmy and pay out of his pocket for us to do this. He wanted the kids to see their dad and be able to visit with him. He was a wonderful man to do this for someone he didn't even know.

"James began to read everything on the trial and he came to the realization that my Jimmy was innocent. He saw that the trial was a farce and Jimmy didn't stand a chance.

"After the trial I got statements from some of the people who testified at his trial which said they had lied on the witness stand, but that didn't do any good either.

"Jimmy Glass said that he had killed those people, but he said that my Jimmy had made him do it. He said Jimmy held a gun on him and just made him kill these people. We know a man who knows all about these murders and he's afraid to talk to clear Jimmy's name. He's afraid of what may happen to his family if he were to speak up. These things happen sometimes, and I don't blame the man for not speaking up. He has to look out for his own family members. It wouldn't be worth it for one of his children to be killed because he tried to clear my Jimmy's name and it wouldn't bring Jimmy back.

"The people weren't very friendly after the trial. Even people that I had known for years would turn and walk away when they saw me coming and wouldn't say anything to me. I had one person say that I should have been able to save my son's life, that I was his mother and it was up to me to take care of him. She was trying to put a guilt trip on me and she was supposed to be my friend. These things hurt me a lot and I decided to change churches. I came across a little country church that I started to go to and the people accepted me as I was. I had done all I could to help my son, God knows I did. I loved my Jimmy and there wasn't anything I wouldn't do to save him.

"Jimmy Glass was mistreated as a child. His parents were alcoholics and the kids made fun of him. I think that's why he did what he did. When he got a gun on the Browns that day and saw they were scared, he loved it. He hated people because of the way he had been treated all his young life and he just killed them. He told someone that he'd had the thrill of his lifetime that night. He felt good inside because he had made someone suffer.

"This is why I fear for my oldest grandson. Because he has that hate inside him. He loved his father and knew he was innocent. I've tried to talk with him and make him see how wrong it is to hate so much. His father wouldn't want him to feel that way. He would want him to go on with his life and make something of himself. My grandchildren are still suffering from all of this. I worry about them something awful. I don't get to see them very often but I've heard how they are being tormented by the other children in school. They yell out, "Your daddy was burned. They burned him up." My grandkids just cry. The oldest boy is fifteen and he hates the system so much for killing his father.

"He wants to beat on these kids who say cruel words to him and his younger sister. I can understand that because sometimes when people make sly remarks to me, I feel like lashing out myself. I hate that they have to go through all this, but kids will be cruel and there's nothing we can do. Some of the kids even call him 'killer Wingo.'

"Their mother is an alcoholic and has been for years. She just refuses to try to help these children, and I can't do it. I don't have any money left over to help them and I just make it by working at the nursing home. I wish I could help them, I really do, but I can't. I'd like to take them away from here where people wouldn't know them or their father. I've begged their mother to do so, but she won't do it.

"I'm not trying to put this lady down because she needs help too, but I just wish she would take more of an interest in the kids.

"My life has been tough since Jimmy was murdered. People still avoid me, not like they used to, but still they do it. My own family is closer to me now and we've stuck together. I cry over Jimmy once in a while, but the Lord has helped me through it. I don't know how I'd have made it if my faith hadn't been so strong.

"I'd like to warn other mothers not to use a court-appointed attorney if your child gets into trouble. If you can't afford one, you might as well forget it because your child will die, like mine did. Not because he is guilty, but because he is poor. Anybody can be in that situation. It doesn't just happen to certain individuals. It can happen to you, it happened to me."

To Those Who
Murdered Jimmy Wingo

by H. Edward Rowe, D.D., President,
Christian Mandate for America

The Jimmy Wingo story has a familiar ring. An arrest under questionable circumstances:

- a small community district attorney seeking to build his image and career by securing convictions;
- a court-appointed defense attorney who is a buddy of the DA;
- a shoddy defense that is more appropriately termed a nondefense;
- intimidated witnesses;
- a conviction based on purely circumstantial and inferential considerations;
- appellate-level reviews of the original trial transcripts, which could not possibly have presented a full factual record of events;
- a futile clemency hearing before a morbid panel of professional deniers whose role is to uphold the system rather than be swayed by compelling evidence;
- rejected reprieves by the Supreme Court and by a gutless wonder governor who talks out of both sides of his mouth with respect to capital punishment, and who would rather have innocent blood dripping from his cruel hands than run the risk of offending the inhabitants of redneckville . . .;
- and all this ending in the murder of a young man within a total vacuum of hard evidence that he had ever in his life been present in the home of the murder victims.

It is a sad day for Louisiana, for America, for civilization, when truth is on the scaffold and wrong on the throne.

Any state that demonstrates a propensity to kill human beings on anything *less* than complete substantive evidence of murder is itself a murderous entity and is not one shade better than the most ruthless and brutal elements of "murder incorporated."

The misuse of human power structures for the self-aggrandizement of

104

killer-tyrants is as old as history. It is also a superserious violation of the moral laws of the Righteous God of the universe, who will ultimately judge and smash every wicked system. The public thought Jimmy Wango was on trial, but from a far more pertinent perspective, Louisiana was on trial in the Wingo case.

Come on, Louisiana, how many more humans are you going to murder on the mere shadow of suspicion supported by nonevidence and based on discredited and or altered testimony?

Come on, you state representatives, when will you ever develop the moral conscience to enact laws strictly forbidding executions pursuant to flimsy though oft-reviewed courtroom trials producing much verbiage and speculation but no real evidence?

Come on, you deputies who threaten witnesses with dire consequences unless they cooperate with you, then program them to give false testimony in the courtroom so as to convict innocent people. Do you really think the Almighty is too blind to see, too deaf to hear your insidious ways — and too lacking in justice to deal with your wickedness in His own way and on His own schedule?

Come on, you judges who appoint inadequate and compromised counsel for the penniless accused, who take bribes from the wealthy, who wink at courtroom improprieties, who suppress truthful testimony and encourage falsehoods, who sit passively while prosecutors brazenly manipulate juries, who uphold those objections which would support deceit and overrule those which would discover truth, who instruct juries so as to predetermine an unjust outcome of trial proceedings. When will you elevate assured evidence and objectively established truth above your own career goals and obligations to the murder machine? Do you really expect the Righteous Judge of the Universe to wink at your sins in that approaching day when you will stand before His bar of justice?

Come on, you appellate and review board panelists who have sold your souls to the most obvious of fabrications, who allow circumstance, conjecture and mere inference to justify your murderous intent, who would rather maintain your power position than exonerate the most innocent of men. Do you really expect your wickedness to flourish forever?

Come on you district attorneys, when will you climb above the selfish and short-sighted goals of career advancement and develop the moral stature to advocate just penalties dictated by impeccably founded truth rather than unconscionable schemes designed to get another scalp on your belt?

Come on, Governor Edwards and Counsel Bill Roberts, you were given all the facts concerning the serious possibility of Mr. Wingo's innocence — yet you chose to run the risk of murdering him rather than grant even a few days' delay so that further investigation of last-minute new evidence could be made. Were you so concerned about covering up the possible crimes of the good ol' boys of the system who allegedly resorted to threats in order to intimidate witnesses into telling lies in court in order to convict Jimmy Wingo?

Come on, Warden Butler, do you really value your job so much as to oversee a possible murder, in spite of all the questions raising facts you heard on the afternoon of June 12?

Come on, veiled executioner, you who prefer to hide behind a pseudonym, you who told the press you don't worry as to whether you're pulling the switch on an innocent man, when will you make it your business to study these cases and to attempt at least to keep your hands clean? When will you decide for a pure conscience in preference of a $400 job that may bring you under the judgment of God for the sin of murder?

Come on, citizens of Louisiana, how long will you be governed by brutal people who, even in the face of changed testimonies and new evidence, prefer to go to bed and sleep serenely while precious people are subjected to the vicious voltage of the electric chair in spite of a total lack of any real evidence of their guilt?

When will you realize that your hands drip with blood too, so long as you remain silent in the face of these outrages? When will you awaken from your slumbers to elect district attorneys whose first commitment is to truth rather than tyranny, to God rather than government?

When will you realize that if Jimmy Wingo can be murdered within a vacuum of evidence and pursuant to a woven fabric of lies and distortions, you can be murdered by the same system?

No, I wouldn't want to share the guilt of the murderous tyranny of Louisiana or any other state. That's why I raise my voice in outrage. I swear eternal hostility to all forms of tyranny that would entertain the slightest risk of murdering the innocent.

Show me the blood of the victim on the hands of the killer before you talk to me about killing the accused.

Yes, I am indignant. From the rooftops of America I shout, *Quit killing on less than total evidence!*

I convey the firm resolution of my soul to fight to my last breath the murderous ways of politicized human systems.

And with all the sincerity of my soul I affirm that I would a million times rather have walked to the electric chair in Jimmy Wingo's shoes than to have stood for one moment of decision in the shoes of Henry Brown, Lawrence J. Hand, Sr., Oris C. Williams, Faye U. Brown, Johnny Jackson, Sr., Edwin W. Edwards, Judge Bill Roberts, Warden Hilton Butler or that anonymous and sleazy man of the slimepit who manipulates the death switch in such an unconcerned manner.

People who murdered Jimmy Wingo, take no comfort in the apparent delay in the implementation of divine justice. It rushes swiftly to meet you at the crossroads of time and eternity. Its coming is inexorable as the tide. Your wicked devices will yet be brought to light. Your evil days are numbered.

Just as Jimmy, his loved ones and friends ran down the clock on that final night, the clock that will deliver your doom ticks away the remaining hours to that inescapable event. The cup of your iniquity will soon overflow. A fate far worse than one you imposed on Jimmy awaits you.

Only genuine repentance and regeneration can spare you now, and it is a consummation devoutly to be recommended.

Benjamin Alers

Vietnam Veteran Convicted of Murder

"I was drafted in 1968 and took my basic training at Fort Jackson, South Carolina. I remember a phrase that the drill sergeants made us cry out, 'Kill! Kill, and kill without mercy.' After training I was sent to Vietnam and was assigned to the First Cavalry Division, Company A, 5th BN 7th Cavalry.

"My baptism of fire was about three weeks after being in country while in the landing zone. We had a ground attack with mortar, rockets and all kinds of automatic weapons. For that action I won my combat infantry badge (CIB) which is awarded to infantrymen who are under enemy fire.

"Most of the time I was in search and destroy missions and did a lot of helicopter combat assaults deep in the jungle area. I met a Cambodian girl about fifteen years old. Her mother would bring her to the soldiers and sell her for five dollars. It was traumatic to me to see such a young girl being sold for money. She spoke perfect English and didn't think anything about going to bed with American soldiers.

"In one of our search and destroy missions, a group of NVA soldiers were walking by and one of them looked right over at us. I asked my squad leader if I could shoot him. I put my M-16 in full automatic and emptied it out on the soldier. The others ran from us and I walked over and saw the boy on the ground with his brains blown out.

"We made a perimeter and stayed pretty close that night. The next day we were attacked by a regiment of NVA soldiers. The fight went on all day and I watched as my friends were taken down.

"They tried to break the perimeter, so I took on the M-60 machine gun and ran to the point. There I fired continually to the advancing enemy. That stopped them for a while. They almost wiped us out before an artillery unit in the landing zone started giving us support fire to help. The NVA then pulled back and left us. I received the Bronze Star, and I believe that they attacked us because of my actions the day before.

"I still remember the jungles, mountains, bomb craters, and unending rains. I left Vietnam in April of 1970 without any physical wounds. However I had malaria and was discharged in November.

"Back in civilian life, I entered work with the Corrections Department as a guard. I began drinking a lot, almost every day. When we had a riot I immediately volunteered to go in as the excitement was a high to me. The psychiatrist said this was a way to extend a combat addiction I brought over from Vietnam. I was suffering from PTSD (post-traumatic stress disorder) and didn't know it. All the actions in my job were viewed in a military way.

"In 1985, during an inmate runaway, I shot one of them in the head. That was considered to be all right by my superiors and the state police as being in the line of duty. My feelings were like it had been in Vietnam when I had to shoot the NVA. I began to drink less alcohol and was told this was part of PTSD. As long as I identified my job as a guard with my combat experiences, I needed less alcohol to keep my high. As a prison guard, my orders were given in the same way that we used in Vietnam, and I always tried to be in the hard areas of the prisons.

"I never accepted office work. The idea was to stay in the areas that gave me the closest remembrances of my grunt times in Nam. My job was the drug that kept my addiction controlled.

"Finally, in 1989, there was an inmate invasion in the institution where I was working. This was the same as the one that we had in 1985. After chasing the men through the swamp area, I shot one of them with a shotgun. This time the DA charged me with murder and I was sent to a psychiatric hospital. I was discharged with PTSD and paranoid personality disorder.

"My attorneys presented a defense of PTSD and having a flashback that impulsed me to shoot. On the other hand, the DA's psychiatrist said that they had found no PTSD on me and I was just a sociopath. They found me guilty of murder and gave me a life sentence. I am in a maximum security unit and attend outpatient treatment in the PTSD unit of the VA hospital. I don't know if I would have been better had I gotten treatment when I first came home from Vietnam or not. I feel that had I not been there, I wouldn't be here now.

Shabaka Waglini
Victim of 14 Years on Death Row

Shabaka Waglini was born Joseph Green Brown in Charleston, South Carolina. He had been convicted for the 1973 murder, robbery, and rape of white Tampa woman. A juror at his trial had sent an affidavit to Shabaka's minister, the Rev. Joe Ingle of the Nashville Southern Coalition on Jails and Prisons, asserting that a jury member had advocated the chair for Shabaka, a former Black Panther, because "that nigger's been nothing but trouble since he came down here, and he'll be trouble until we get him off the streets."

Only 15 hours before Shabaka's appointment with death, a three-judge panel of the federal circuit court of appeals in Atlanta stayed the execution on grounds that the case merited further examination. Shabaka returned to his cell and began to petition for a new trial.

In the years that followed, ugly details came to light. During the first trial, the prosecutor had concealed FBI evidence showing that the fatal bullet could not have come from Shabaka's gun. The prosecutor had allowed a crucial witness to lie while also misleading the jury in his closing arguments.

"I was born in Charleston, South Carolina, and in 1966 I went to Orlando, Florida, where I was to live for most of my life. I'm sure that my being charged with the murder and rape of Mrs. Barksdale was a deliberate and intentional thing, brought by the police department and the Hillsborough County State Attorney's Office simply to frame me. Since I was black and they needed someone, I was perfect for the part.

"I had a court-appointed attorney because I didn't have the money to hire one. He was just three years out of law school and had only tried three previous cases before a jury, and none of them were capital cases.

·"After the trial, the main prosecution witness recanted his testimony and insisted on telling the truth in spite of threats of a life sentence from the judge and the prosecutor. After many years, the state finally administered a polygraph test. The results supported the witness's statement that he had lied during the trial.

"I became friends with Deborah Fins of the Legal Defense Fund in

New York and she found another attorney for me. He wouldn't have been my choice, if I had one. He had just resigned as the U.S. Attorney for the State of Connecticut, and had never handled a capital case either. He also believed in the death penalty, but when he came to see me I liked him. I asked him one question, could he fight? He never did respond, just sort of smiled and there was something in that smile. The smile was not just on his face but in his eyes, and there was something about it that told me here was a man that I could trust.

"It came up that he was a man that I could trust and we stuck it out and worked very well together. It was the first time he had a chance to see capital punishment up close. I came down to 15 hours before my execution when I got the stay.

"When my death warrant was signed by Governor Graham in 1983, my mother suffered some serious medical problems. Today she is still paralyzed from them. I had no way of assuring her that I was going to be all right and it was too much for her. I tried to tell her that these people would never kill me, and it was something that I had to believe. I think it was at this point my attorney changed his mind on the death penalty.

"When he read the transcript of my trial, he was in awe of the injustices he saw.

"I guess most of my emotions were of anger. The day before the execution they came to the cell. The cell was located about thirty feet from the electric chair and you had to stay in that cell for an average of twenty-three days. There are only two ways to get out of that cell. One is to get a stay of execution; the other is to take that walk to the chair.

"The guards came in to measure me for a burial suit and it was then that I blew my cool. They made it seem like a ritual, so mechanical like I was an inanimate object or something, not a living human being. I was determined at that point to let them know that I was not just a ritual, but a human being. I was still alive, breathing, and I would demand respect. I lashed out physically, and they responded in like manner. I lost four teeth in that altercation.

"I was full of anger. Anger at being treated in such a manner, anger at my mother's heart attack, anger at the world. We got the stay but it was given very grudgingly. The ballistic reports from the FBI showed the bullet that was taken from the body did not physically match the chamber of the gun that I had. We didn't even have the original autopsy report. We had the report of the medical examiner first on the scene, and this report said that the assailants had blood groups AB and B. I am type A+ The state knew this and also knew the time of death was fixed at between 5:30 and 8:00 in the evening. At the trial, the state maintained the crime took place around noon.

"We also found out from inmates that the key witness who testified not only didn't know about the crime, but was taught and trained by the police and prosecution. He was taken out of the jail every day and led around the scene of the crime, shown pictures of where the body lay and everything. This evidence was found by us and I turned to Tom, the local counsel, and said, 'What I like about you white people is that you always like to write things down! Yes, man, you always write things down and they come back to haunt you.'

"Today I have anger, frustration, bitterness and hatred. Those feelings will always be there. I choose to let that show, and I choose to let people know of my feelings. I have to in order to survive. I dictate my own emotions. When I was released, I had nothing but seventy-five cents in my pocket. I gave away all my law books to the others on the row, and I only had the seventy-five cents with which to make a phone call. I called Tom, my lawyer, who is based in St. Petersburg, and asked him to come and pick me up. In Florida, like other states, when an inmate is freed, he is given a suit and one hundred dollars and a ticket back to their hometown. Since I had been at the county jail the last couple of months, I was given nothing.

"When I stepped out of the jail, I was met with reporters and was blinded by the lights from the TV station cameras that had been waiting for me. I don't feel free; I am no longer restrained by bars, but that's as far as it goes. During one interview a reporter asked me to smile. I told him I wasn't going to be cute, I wasn't going to smile for the camera. It's too serious an issue, the death penalty, and that's what I'm about. I say what I have to say even though there's a lot of people who don't want to hear it. No one owns Shabaka, I'm not a paid public servant. I'm myself, and I'll always be myself. I'm going to say what I believe in my heart and what I believe is right.

"I have more respect for the Nazis than I do for the Americans. At least the Nazis had the courage to say, 'I'm going to kill you, you and you because I don't like the color of your eyes, the color of your hair or skin.' They don't give you a fair trial, the right to appeal and all the mockery and trickery that we have. What makes us any different?

"I've had people ask me, 'Mr. Brown, we understand your situation and we sympathize with you.' I say, 'Don't sympathize with me.' They say, 'If someone kills your mother, can't they answer for it with capital punishment?' And I always respond with, 'What if it were your mother who killed my mother? Would you still be for capital punishment?' I get no response to this question. Capital punishment not only has hurt me, but it has hurt my family. I say, 'You people have already killed a member of my family. You killed my brother as sure as if you took a gun and aimed and pulled the trigger.'

"In 1970 my brother Willie needed a kidney transplant. He lived in

Georgia and the doctors contacted me and came to Florida's state prison. I was examined and our kidneys matched perfectly. State officials in Tallahassee said that I could not be transported because of security reasons. The doctors then said they would bring Willie up to Gainesville, Florida, which is located twenty-two miles from the prison. Again I was denied to go and give my kidney. Nine days later, Willie died because he didn't have a kidney transplant. So, in a sense, the state of Florida killed my brother. They killed him.

"Every time I go and see my mother and see the condition she's in, I feel hatred. I hurt when I see my family suffer and I take offense. I can deal with what they did to me, but when you touch the ones I love and care about, I take offense. The families are also victims because they are being ostracized by society, exiled, and that is sad.

"There are victims all the way around. Society teaches that when something violent happens to us we should seek revenge, but I always ask the question about who out there will volunteer themselves to be a sacrificial lamb for me, so I can release fourteen years of anger and frustration? I get no volunteers. Society tells me I shouldn't act that way and I should suppress it. I have to suppress my outrage because, you see, they have no program in society for people like myself.

"I've got to live the rest of my life with the knowledge that I had a brother who's no longer with us because I was denied the right to give him one of my kidneys. I don't care what happens to me. I'm a survivor and always have been, but when you touch that which is precious to me, then you can say Shabaka and you are enemies. I'm not through with Hillsborough County, Florida, not by a long shot. I'm going to bring them down."

Shabaka spends his free time discussing the death penalty. He has testified before the Connecticut legislature as they debated a new death penalty bill, spoken to the press in numerous states, appeared on radio and talk shows, and addressed a benefit for the Southern Coalition on Jails and Prisons. He says that his major concern is for those men and women still on death row. He is doing all he can to work for the end to this ultimate punishment, a punishment that he knows came within 15 hours of taking one innocent man's life.

Many apologists will say that Shabaka's release after 14 years on death row shows the system works. The system failed. What worked was a dedicated group of death penalty monitors and attorneys. Without committed volunteer attorneys, Shabaka would likely be dead today. Evidence of his innocence would not have been found, and people would have thought the system worked, because it had convicted, sentenced to death, and killed the guilty party, when in fact it would have killed an innocent man.

Marie Deans

Death Penalty Legal Defense Coordinator

(Speech given by Marie Deans at the August 1987 meeting of the American Corrections Congress in New Orleans, Louisiana.)

First I want to tell you where I'm coming from — mainly because too many corrections officials make easy and inaccurate assumptions about people who do the work I do.

I am the death penalty legal defense coordinator in Virginia. Under grants from law schools and the Virginia Law Foundation, I track all death cases, assist and resource appointed attorneys, whether private or public defenders. Through other grants and donations, I recruit volunteer attorneys to represent those under sentence of death and serve as coordinator of the cases. In that capacity, I have constant contact with the attorneys, the men on the row (we have no women at this time), their families, corrections personnel, and chaplains who work with death row inmates.

In the last five executions in Virginia, I have been in the death house with the men until a few minutes before they were killed. During the time they are in the death house — at least fifteen days in Virginia — I also work with them, their families, and their attorneys on a daily basis. Occasionally, I also work with the victim's family.

Before I came to Virginia, I worked for a number of years in South Carolina and was with two men killed there.

So I've been in the death house with seven men just before they were killed, and I've also been with several who received last-minute stays.

I am also a member of a murder victim's family. My mother-in-law, Penny, was murdered by an escaped convict in 1972, and I am the founder of a national organization of murder victims' families that opposes the death penalty in every case.

One of the reasons we oppose it is that studies from all over the world, including contiguous states with and without the death penalty in this country, show that if the death penalty has any effect on the homicide rate, it is to increase it.

It is clear that support for the death penalty is based on assumption rather than on fact. The facts all go the other way. It is also clear that the death penalty is a very expensive bogus "solution" in that it likely causes the deaths of additional innocent victims, depletes the resources of the states, the courts, the criminal justice system, and the corrections system, and that it serves as a red herring that keeps us from seeking effective solutions to homicide.

On the other hand, it is the cheapest ticket any politician can punch to further his career. There are over a hundred families in our organization, most of whom do work similar to mine or work in states with no death penalty to be sure those states remain abolitionist. We do this work because we have been there. We know what murder leaves behind, and we deeply resent cheap, emotional, unknowing support of the death penalty which likely creates additional families like ours and blocks efforts to find effective solutions, and we resent our pain being exploited to support this red herring.

Because we are exploited and used as pawns in what we call the politics of death, we recognize others who are exploited, victimized, and used as pawns. Although there are many people who have no sympathy for you, and many in our organization who have difficulty forgiving you, most of us see you as pawns, as exploited, and as being victimized. The problem for us comes because you are apparently willing pawns, while victims' families have no choice. Another problem is that we identify very strongly with the families of men and women on death row. While you may rationalize a difference between state killing and individual killing — calling one murder and one execution — we know that the impact on both families is the same. If there is a difference it is that for the families of those who are killed by the state, it is worse, for they have to watch and wait helplessly as their loved one faces a predetermined death date. They live for years anticipating a killing and then live through it and then live with the aftermath. God knows what all the aftermath will entail. In Virginia alone there are seven children whose fathers were killed in Virginia's death chamber.

No matter what the circumstances of a particular victimization, the common wound is the psychological one of being treated like an object rather than as a human being.

In this case, it begins with the murder of an innocent human being whom the murderer treated like an object. That act is not only dehumanizing to the victim, it is also dehumanizing for the murderer.

The death penalty consistently fails to do anything to rectify that act in any way. In fact, prisons, as they are today, fail as well because neither do anything to hold the murderer responsible for his or her act of murder. So long as the murderer does not acknowledge his responsibility by seeing his or her victim as a human being and recognizing the humanity of his or her victim, society's punishment is a useless act of vengeance. That is not to say that some murderers do not come to recognize their victims' humanity and accept responsibility for what they have done. Some do, but they do it in spite of the death penalty and prison.

The dehumanization goes on. The victim's family are treated like objects by law enforcement and the courts, as sensational objects by the press and community, as political fodder by politicians. Certainly turning a human being into a conductor of electricity is dehumanizing, but the dehumanization begins again by law enforcement and the courts and goes on once that person reaches death row. Dehumanizing him or her then dehumanizes the family, because they are too often viewed as mere extensions of the inmate. Their perception is that corrections people view them as murderers as well.

The people, including the governors, treat you as objects, and you are very helpful in that process, because you treat one another as objects. Your treatment of the people on the row and their families ends up dehumanizing you as well. I'm not saying you are being intentionally cruel. What I am saying is that you don't realize that you are being cruel, you are following procedures.

The mother of one of our clients drove all the way from Michigan to see her son and was strip-searched for a noncontact visit. When she was told she was going to be strip-searched and she objected, she was told she could leave without seeing her son. The ACLU investigated this incident and found out the only reason they could find for the strip-search was the guard thought the man was a pain. The woman was in poor health and had never caused the prison one bit of trouble. That is diffuse punishment, and it is dehumanizing to everyone involved.

The psychologist Theodor Teik said about war, "To kill one's enemies, bomb their cities, destroy their women and children and property in cold blood, emotionally indifferent, would be monstrous. Imagine yourself a soldier attacking Nazis. Is it possible to drive a bayonet through a human body in a mood of benevolent detachment? How abominable it would be to kill because of some well-considered reason. It would be atrocious to wipe out lives without passion, hate, or vindictiveness, simply because it is a useful thing to do."

But with the exception of bombing, this is exactly what society is now demanding from corrections officials.

How do you go on doing their dirty work and acting like nothing happened? You do it by justifying the death penalty, by rationalizing your roles, by dehumanizing yourselves, by getting involved in the details and the ritual. You try to turn yourselves into efficient technicians of death.

The problem is that killing is not an academic matter. It is a human matter. And just as murder is dehumanizing for the murderer, state killing is a dehumanizing act for those who kill by decree.

You can, of course, deny that. You can tell me that I've misunderstood all the guards, execution squad members, counselors, assistant wardens, wardens, directors and commissioners who have talked with me privately. You can agree with the private citizen in the audiences I speak to when I tell them they have no right to demand that you carry out their filthy, dirty work and they respond, "Hey, they knew when they took the job. They made the choice to get involved in executions. If they don't like pulling the switch, they can leave. Plenty more where they come from." They think you are as expendable as the people on death row.

I've learned a lot working in prisons, and one thing I've learned is that machismo isn't restricted to one side of the bars, so you can tell me I'm wrong about correctional officials being victimized by the death penalty, but I'll tell you what I hear if you do. I hear denial. Murder victims' families go through denial, too, and denial is an amazingly strong human defense. It isn't strong enough though.

Now and then I run across corrections officials who genuinely don't care, who really are efficient technicians of death. I'm a lot more afraid of those people than I am of the people on death row.

I'll tell you something else I hear in the rhetoric. I hear fear—fear of losing your jobs, fear of going over the edge, fear of retribution.

Those are legitimate fears, but you do have choices. One is to go on carrying out state killings. Another is to leave individually and quietly. Many have made that choice. Another is to leave, but say why. There is another choice, and that is to take a professional stand together. The truth is you don't have to be death technicians. The truth is you are responsible for your actions, too. Whatever you do, I hope you won't lie to yourselves and others and say you have no other choice.

In my opinion, corrections will never be a true profession until you claim it as a profession. Until then, it will be a political pawn subject to whatever crackpot wind blows out of the latest party caucus or politician's ambition, including killing Velma Barfield for Senate seat.

There are almost two thousand people on death row in this country, and they are adding about two hundred a year. Eighty-six of those have been killed. You have thousands to go, and believe me the courts are cranking open the floodgates. But they are still going to let the people on death row sit for years waiting, and you are in charge of holding them for years and then killing them as long as you decide that is your job.

Maria Dicks

Daughter of Death Row Inmate

"I'm eleven years old and for as long as I can remember my mother and I have gone to the prison to visit with my daddy every week. My grandmother adopted me when I was born but I call her Mommy because she is the only mother I ever knew. My mother didn't want me and was going to give me away.

"When we visit with my daddy, we go into a cage with a table and have Cokes and candy while we visit. Some people don't realize that I know the state wants to kill my daddy. I don't know how they can say it is wrong for someone to kill someone, then they turn around and do the very same thing. My daddy never hurt anyone in his life, but they still want to kill him.

"We play cards when we visit and I win a lot of the time. I love my daddy so much and he's so good to me. When I was little, he gave me his color television, the only one he had. He told my mother that he still had his, that he had bought me that one. Then a long time later we found out he was using a small black and white one. He didn't care that he couldn't watch television in color, he just wanted to give me something of his because he loves me so much. That's the way my daddy is, always thinking of someone else even though he goes without things a lot of the time.

"We used to live in a mobile home park and I had a best friend there. One day I gave her a box of clothes that I had outgrown. They were all good clothes, but the next day she brought them back to me. Her grandmother told her she couldn't have them because my daddy was in prison. Then her mother said that my daddy deserved what he got, that he was no good. I was so mad at her, but I couldn't talk back to an adult. I didn't tell Mommy for a long time because I didn't want her to get in a fight with Vallie's mother. I don't know why some people can be so mean to other people just because they have someone in prison. They just don't care that he's innocent.

"Some of the kids at school used to make fun of me because my daddy was in prison and I was sick a lot. Most of the time I said I was sick so I wouldn't have to go to school but then Mommy put me in the church school. The kids there are so nice to me, and some of them even write to some boys on death row.

For Father's Day this year I bought a real gold chain for Daddy to wear. He loved it and gave me a big hug and kiss. My best friend Kandy goes to the prison with me sometimes to visit with Daddy. Her mother lets her go and we have a good time. We usually go to Shoney's after our visit so we can eat before heading home.

"Sometimes I hear my mommy crying and I cry too. It hurts that my daddy can't be home with us. It hurts to think that someone wants to kill him and we can't do anything to get him out of that place. I ask Mommy why. Why do these people want to kill him? That won't help anybody to kill my daddy and it won't bring anybody back to life.

"We pray every day for my daddy and I know that Jesus will hear our prayers. Jesus was put on death row and they executed him for something he didn't do, so I know he loves my daddy. Another man committed the murder, but they said my daddy went in the store with him. Chief will never get to heaven because he won't tell the truth and free my daddy. Jesus tells us to forgive those who do wrong to us, but I don't think I can forgive Chief for what he has done to my daddy and us.

"I wouldn't trade my daddy for the president or anybody else. I'm proud that he's mine and I know I have the best daddy in the world. But Jesus will save him and one day he will come home to live with Mommy and me and that will be the happiest day of my life."

Anthony Guest

Death Row Inmate

"I've wanted to somehow convey to you the sensations, the atmospheric pressure, you might say, of what it is like to be a victim of the death penalty. That doesn't adequately say what I mean to say, what it's like to be on death row. To be locked up so long, it's difficult to remember exactly what you were accused of to get here. So long your fantasies of the free world are no longer easily distinguishable from what you know the free world is really like. So long that being free is exactly identical to a free man's dream of heaven. To die and go to the free world.

"I've lived here on death row for the past eight years. Death row to me resembles Dachau and Buchenwald. This place brings out the very best in humans or destroys them entirely. None here are unaffected. None who leave here leave as they came. If I leave here alive, I'll leave nothing behind, but I can't say that I'll leave here normal either. I try to understand my surroundings, and I've asked myself, as I do about all the other abstracts of life, 'Why?' Why does a system encompass the needs and requirements of all, or, to be realistic, the majority? Why are the terms so harsh, the price of defeat so high? What is it that causes men/women to become power-made and deify exploitation and mendacity and the compatible, harmonious things of nature?

"I am by nature a gentle man, and I love the simple things in life. Good food, an expressive book, music, and pretty women. I used to enjoy a walk in the rain, a summer day in the park. But reality is a powerful, sometimes crushing entity. It overwhelms every sense we have [except] the pain and sorrow.

"Even our wives and girlfriends, with whom we have shared the tenderest moments and most delicate affections, leave us after a while, put us down, cut us clean, and treat us like they hate us. Won't even write letters, send a Christmas card, or a dollar for a pack of cigarettes or a tube of toothpaste now and then. To maintain a hold on the ideas and sentiments of civilization in such circumstances is probably impossible.

"If we had any purpose in life, it is all going to waste. Here in this huge, dark, streaming pit of death row, men are herded together like cattle, most of them with nothing to do. All the senses and imagination, sensibilities and emotions, sorrows and desires, and hopes and ideas are forced in upon themselves, bound inward by an iron ring of frustration that hems them in with its four insurmountable walls. In this huge cauldron, natural gifts, wisdom, love, music, science, poetry are stamped down and their souls are destroyed by misery and degradation, wiped out, washed from the register of the living, dehumanized.

"That part of me which wanders through my mind and never feels or sees actual objects, but which lives in and moves through my passions and my emotions, experiences this world as a horrible nightmare. I'm talking now about the men in my dreams. The one that appears in my dreams as me. The one that is both the subject and object of all those symbols.

"But if you do that for too long, you lose yourself. Because there is something helpless and weak and innocent, something like an infant deep inside us all that really suffers in ways we would never permit an insect to suffer. That is how death row is tearing me up inside. It hurts every day. Every day takes me further from my life. And I am not even conscious of how my dissolution is coming about. Therefore, I cannot stop it.

"This year my mother and niece and a lady from their church were traveling along the interstate heading to Memphis, Tennessee, for a church prayer meeting when the van they were riding in broke down on the road. The minister got out and starting walking to a town in order to seek help. My mother and niece and the other lady waited in the van for the minister to get back. Another van with a drunk driver behind the wheel came barreling up the highway and ran into the back of the van they were waiting in. All three were killed, and the system says we on death rows are animals. Because of my death sentence, I wasn't allowed to see my mother one last time. I couldn't go to the funeral to say goodbye. There are so many things that we on death row aren't allowed to do. If I had been sentenced to a term of imprisonment, no matter how long the sentence, I would have been allowed to say goodbye to my family.

"It's too bad society can't see that the death penalty is wrong, that it only creates more victims. My family members are innocent, and yet they are victims also. They will lose their loved one to a murder."

James Earl Ray

Victim of Society

On April 4, 1968, at the Lorraine Motel in Memphis, Tennessee, a sniper's bullet struck and killed Dr. Martin Luther King, Jr., the most charismatic leader of America's 20 million blacks. The next day, as if on cue, flames roared above the ghettos in dozens of American cities and on millions of TV screens around the world.

A week later, the Equal Opportunity in Housing bill, a racially based act that would create a trillion-dollar market for the lenders of credit, was rushed through Congress after years of stalemate.

In what the press called "the most intense manhunt in its history," the FBI searched worldwide for Dr. King's assassin. Two months after the murder, James Earl Ray, an escaped convict from the Missouri State Prison, was arrested in London and brought to Memphis, Tennessee, where he was confined in a torture chamber for nine months until coerced by his lawyer into pleading guilty. He was sentenced to 99 years in prison.

Did James Earl Ray really assassinate Martin Luther King, Jr.? Surveys indicate as many as 80 percent of the American people don't believe he did. Even black leaders close to Dr. King have expressed doubts that Ray was the murderer or had any knowing involvement in the homicide.

Of course the matter could be solved easily in a jury trial, where all the evidence would be reviewed by 12 citizens. James Earl Ray has wanted a jury trial for 19 years. But the state and federal governments have strenuously objected to trying the King case by jury.

One can search for solutions in books, but of the dozen or so volumes about the King assassination, most have been written by parties under some kind of contract with a government agency. Naturally, they support the government's position, which strongly contradicts all available evidence.

Many citizens, including historical scholars, have been fearful that the truth about Dr. King's death might be in danger of never being known, especially since a federal court has ordered all government intelligence documents related to Dr. King and the assassination put under seal for 50 years in the National Archives.

But truth is not so easily stifled. After years of painstaking research under the most incredible handicaps imaginable, the world's most authoritative known source on the King assassination has at last rendered the definitive statement. And now all Americans, and the world, can judge for themselves whether or not Dr. King was murdered by the man whom the government and the press credit with the deed.

"After I had served time in Leavenworth, I had a bus ticket to Kansas City, furnished by the government, and about fifty dollars earned for prison work. I was required by the federal regulation to reside in that city until the conditional release expired. I checked into a hotel and reported directly to the parole officer. I would check in with him personally or via phone every day and give details of my efforts to find a job.

"I went to the local baker's union, introducing myself as a just-released prisoner inquiring about a job. The next day he called for me to report for work in a local bakery. At the time of the call, I was reporting to the parole officer and the job went to somebody else, and I received no further offers from the union.

"I knew if I didn't transfer back to St. Louis, I'd be right back in Leavenworth, so I used what little money I had left and bought two alligator clips and some electrical wire. After dark, I found a used car lot and hot-wired an old clunker and headed for St. Louis. At daybreak, five miles from the city, the engine blew so I went on foot.

"For the first few months I worked at several part-time jobs. I decided I wanted to leave the United States but there were no handbooks available on how to become a former U.S. citizen; the only intelligence on the issue was what I could gather from conversation and common sense. I went to Canada but couldn't work without a card, like our social security cards. So I returned to St. Louis again where I met an ex-con, James Owens.

"James Owens and I were charged in the robbery of a Kroger supermarket in 1959. The arrest took place a few minutes after James had been taken into custody. Although the modus operandi in carrying out the arrest was a rather routine operation for police officers in St. Louis, it didn't conform to the procedure one sees on the television tube, where the officer reads the suspect his prerogatives, including the right to remain silent. Instead, one of the arresting detectives grabbed me from behind and commenced to pistol-whipping me about the head, yelling, 'Where's the other bastard?' A nearby occupant stuck his head out of a door and started to inquire about all the racket. The detective fired a shot at him. The bullet lodged in the door frame near the tenant's head.

"During the trial my attorney attempted to subpoena the tenant who'd been shot at. The proprietor of the apartment building informed the attorney that minutes after the shooting incident the tenant, who had only recently moved in, was seen hastily leaving the premises with his personal belongings in tow. There was no forwarding address. The tenant probably assumed he'd moved into a rowdy neighborhood. He never knew he'd been fired upon by a police officer, since the detective was in plainclothes.

"I was given a twenty-year sentence, and James received a seven-year sentence in exchange for a guilty plea. After seven months, I decided it was time to consider an escape. My job in the cleaning plant offered a reasonable opportunity. I took cover behind some boxes until everyone left. I started to make a makeshift ladder with shelving. Dragging the ladder behind, I crawled toward the clothing shop about fifty feet away. I put the ladder up to the wall and then stepped on the first rung, and it felt secure. I was halfway to the top when the ladder began creaking, then collapsed under my weight at the spot where I had spliced the boards together. The guards didn't hear the racket, so I went back to the cleaning plant for a backup plan.

"This time I took some pipes and made a makeshift ladder and tried again. The pipes fell, and this time when I returned to the cleaning plant, a half dozen guards invaded the building and spotted me. I was charged with attempted escape.

"At about eight o'clock in the morning of April 23, 1967, I entered the kitchen. After eating a dozen eggs (I didn't know where my next meal would be coming from), I waited for my accomplice's prearranged signal indicating the coast was clear to enter the bread storage room. Directly I got the sign.

"Inside the room everything was ready. I climbed into the breadbox, covered myself with the false bottom, and the loaves were stacked upon me. It was unsettling being compressed into a small space. Then the truck began moving toward the last barrier to the outside.

"As soon as the truck started picking up speed, I began pushing the loaves away, lifting myself out of the box. I slipped out of the prison clothes and into a black pair of pants, with the truck well on the way. The truck stopped for a moment and I leapt to the ground. Not wanting to look like a desperado, I casually waved toward the driver when I straightened up, as if I'd just been a civilian hitching a ride. I headed for St. Louis and a friend I knew there. He was Jack Gawron, or Catman. He was a police informant, although I didn't know that until the following year when the government tried to use him to solve the Rev. Martin Luther King, Jr. homicide.

"I found a job under the name of John Rayns, a name that I had a social security number to match. After a month I purchased a car for a hundred dollars. I needed the car mainly to obtain identification papers; with car title in hand, I took and passed a driver's license examination, this after giving the examiner a ten spot. I felt it safe to move about in areas where authorities might request identification.

"It was at this time I phoned my brother Jerry and we arranged to meet.

Jerry told me that the FBI had briefly questioned him about my possible location. (It didn't hit me then, but I wonder now: Why was the FBI probing so deeply into the escape of a two-bit crook? Did my vulnerability and psychological profile make me a leading candidate to be placed in a desired circumstance at a desired time?)

"I moved back to Canada in June of 1967 and called Catman Gawron. I needed to ask him for a favor. I had to get a particular family member to rent a post office box under an assumed name so I could correspond with them from Canada or wherever. I met with Catman and he agreed to contact the family member about the post office box. He agreed to get me a pistol from a fence we both knew. Now that I was armed, I figured that if the lack of funds situation became untenable in Canada, I could remedy the condition without intruding on a legitimate business operation. (But what I didn't figure on was that the Catman would one day inform the FBI that I had on July 13th, before leaving East St. Louis, robbed the nearby Bank of Alton in Alton, Illinois.)

"I then drove to Montreal and rented an efficiency at the Har–K Apartments. It was here that I used the name of Eric S. Galt for the first time as an alias. I tried to see about getting a Canadian passport but was told I would need a sworn affidavit from a Canadian citizen attesting that he had known me to be a Canadian citizen for the past two years. I didn't like all the red tape and thought there might be a more efficient way to lay hands on a travel document.

"One of the bars I patronized was the Neptune Tavern. One day a man of Spanish accent sat at my table. He said his name was Raoul. Little did I know that Raoul would one day involve me in the murder of the Rev. Martin Luther King, Jr. Had he been steered to me? I can't say for sure. I had been in the bar many times asking about documents of bogus travel. He may very well have been assigned to me by parties that had been watching me ever since my postescape contacts with the Catman.

"Over the next few days I had further meetings with Raoul. The result: he would help me with the travel documents conditioned on my assisting him. He needed help in moving some material across the Canadian border into the United States. I accepted.

"I was to assist him in getting some materials into Mexico also. He was to get me a passport and then I could return to Canada and utilize the bogus passport to depart for Australia or Europe.

"The first run I was to wait at the Windsor train station and he would contact me. I did wait and he appeared. He got in the front seat and we moved to a side street. After I parked, he moved around into the back seat where he removed three plastic bags from his case; they appeared to be three by six inches. He concealed the bags in the seat springs and returned to the front seat and directed me to the tunnel that would take us into

Detroit. Before we got to the tunnel entrance, Raoul had me stop the car so he could get out. He would take a taxi the rest of the way and I would pick him up on the American side.

"I gave him a few minutes to get a cab, then drove through the tunnel and picked him up on the other side of the United States Customs House. He directed me to park on a side street, where he removed the packages and said we would do the operation again. Apparently, he'd been testing me on this first run through.

"The next run Raoul had me cross over the bridge rather than take the tunnel. When I drew near the Customs House on the United States side, I noticed several cars being detained waiting to be searched. Recalling a television set I'd recently purchased in Montreal was sitting in the backseat, I decided to declare it just to be safe. When I did, the officer waved me into another lane where they shook down cars.

"The officer searched the Plymouth meticulously, but just as he got to the back seat, something very suspicious happened. Many years later I would recall this incident to the House Select Committee, hoping that someone in government familiar with customs practices or the way the CIA operates might shed light on what really was going on here. Of course, the politicians passed right over it. Here's what transpired: just as the first customs officer got to the backseat area, a second officer approached and informed the first that he would complete the search. The first officer walked away, and the second abruptly terminated the shakedown. Then he assessed me a four dollar import tax on the television set.

"When I picked up Raoul, he asked about the delay and I told him what had happened. We parked and he again took out the packages, apparently satisfied. Nothing was said about another rerun. Instead, he mentioned something about a problem in getting a passport for me. He gave me a telephone number for me to contact him with. It was a number in New Orleans, Louisiana. He told me to go to Birmingham and pick up a letter at the post office under the name of Eric Galt.

"On August 26, I went to the main office of the post office in Birmingham and picked up a letter from him. It instructed me to meet him on a certain date.

"On that meeting he instructed me to get a car for a project he had in mind. After a couple of days of shopping around I found a 1966 pale yellow Mustang. Raoul gave me the money to get the car, although he didn't much like the pale yellow color. When the Mustang later figured in the King homicide, the press universally described it as "white." Why not pale yellow? Could it be that white had greater psychological value in prejudicing public opinion against the accused killer of a black figure?

"Raoul gave me some money to live on and a list of things to pick up for him when we were to meet for a drive into Mexico. He got the phone number in the lobby of the rooming house I was staying in so he could contact me. Then I had to get a driver's license in the name of Eric Galt.

"In late September I received a call from Raoul mentioning our upcoming trip to Mexico. He wanted me to call him in New Orleans. When I called I reached his intermediary again, who indicated he'd been expecting my call. I told him that I had everything done with the exception of the movie camera and telephoto lens which Raoul had instructed me to get. He said that I should phone him when it arrived.

"After several days and the equipment did not arrive, I called again to find out what to do. I was told that Raoul had already left for Mexico and I was to go there and check into a certain hotel and wait until contacted.

"With some time on my hands, I tried to identify the number that Raoul had given me. Matching the numbers, I found it listed under the name of Herman A. Thompson. I then drove into Mexico and checked into the hotel where I met with Raoul. He said we were going to do the same type operation as we had done in Canada. We left the motel and followed through on the procedure as he had outlined. After I picked him up on the U.S. side of the border, we drove for ten blocks and he motioned me to pull over and park behind another automobile. He got out and got a tire out of the trunk and put it in the Mustang. He directed me to go back and when they were searching my car, to give the Mexican customs agents exactly one dollar apiece grease money. No more, no less.

"The car Raoul had taken the spare tire from was parked in the motel's entrance driveway when I got there. First in left profile, then frontally as he turned to face us, I could see a dark male in the driver's seat whose nose suggested Indian extraction. Years later, I would identify this individual by name, establishing that he had acted as a bagman in political assassinations in Argentina.

"Before leaving the motel the next day he transferred the loaded tire from his car back into the trunk of the Mustang. I noticed the chalk marks were still there. We made it over the border and Raoul passed my car and pulled over to the side of the road. I pulled in beside of the car and he told me that he still hadn't gotten the passport for me. He gave me two thousand dollars and told me to keep in touch and keep checking general delivery at the Los Angeles post office.

"As I watched Raoul and his passenger drive away, I felt somewhat relieved. An isolated stretch of Mexican road would have been a most convenient spot for them to eliminate permanently whatever legal threat I might someday pose to them.

"I would learn in later years the Mexican federal police had me under surveillance while I was in Acapulco. It's been established that a Mexican police officer named Ramon del Rio severed from the registration book in the San Francisco Motel the information I had provided when registering. Apparently no official explanation has been given for this action. Rather, the government has classified it.

"In the meantime, others appeared to have been laying the groundwork for the assault on the Rev. Martin King, Jr. In March, someone representing himself as Eric S. Galt telephoned the Alabama State Highway Patrol office in Birmingham. The party claimed he had lost his license and requested a duplicate. Prosecution-oriented author Gerold Frank would claim that the duplicate license had been ordered by me after losing the original to the muggers. My wallet had not only contained the license, but also the certificate of title to the Mustang. Surely if I'd lost the latter I would have applied for a duplicate of it too. I would have requested it be sent to my new address in Los Angeles. The truth about this duplicate license is contained in government files which the United States Department of Justice has apparently classified.

"On March 17, I went to Birmingham and called Raoul and his intermediary answered and told me that Raoul would meet me at our old contact place. I picked Raoul up there and by evening we were in Atlanta. He gave me directions to an area of the city where he suggested that I find an apartment to rent. I did find one just off Peachtree Street. Raoul stayed in the car while I went in and rented a room.

"The next day Raoul spoke about getting a foreign and domestic rifle. We drove to Birmingham and I got a room at the motel. We checked the Yellow Pages for sporting goods stores and I called and asked if they had the type of guns we were looking for. Raoul gave me some money and I drove out alone and told the clerk that I was looking for a good deer rifle for my brother-in-law. Later, Mr. Wood would misrepresent brother-in-law as brother, which mistake the press would use in an attempt to demonstrate that Raoul was a purely imaginary cover I had invented to hide a conspiracy with my brother to assassinate Dr. King.

"I gave a name of a friend of my brother that popped into my mind. I got the rifle and went back to the motel. Raoul said he was going to New Orleans and I was to bring the rifle to Memphis, Tennessee, and he would contact me later. He said some gun buyers were going to meet him.

"On March 30 I stayed in a motel near Decatur, Alabama. On the 31st, I stayed in the area of Florence and Tuscumbia, still in Alabama. April 1st I stopped overnight at a motel near Corinth, Mississippi, and on April 2nd I checked into the Desoto Motel on Highway 51, about two blocks south of the Tennessee border and the city limits of Memphis.

"A decade later, however, my location for April 2 would become controversial. The House Select Committee and the FBI testimony would insist that I didn't depart from Atlanta until April 3rd, upon which day, according to them, I rushed off to Memphis in a racist frenzy after reading in the Atlanta newspapers about Dr. King's return to Memphis.

"But in October 1974 investigator Harold Wiesberg would go to the Desoto in connection with a habeas corpus hearing in the King homicide case and interview the maid and manager. Both witnesses would testify I was there, not in Atlanta, on April 2nd. (The manager was killed shortly after this interview, incidentally.) The Desoto people also told Mr. Wiesberg that two FBI agents had been there asking about me shortly after the assassination.

"The Justice Department would deny having any records for my location on that day. And since the House Select Committee would sequester in the National Archives 185 cubic feet of its assassination file at the conclusion of the committee's investigation, all the records that didn't support the government's version of the Martin Luther King, Jr. homicide. Thus, my location for April 2 can not be discovered from committee files. The next day, April 3rd, I drove to Lamar Avenue in Memphis and checked into the New Rebel Motel, in accord with Raoul's instructions. I parked the Mustang right at the door.

"Early that evening Raoul showed up and after making sure I had brought the rifle, he briefed me on what would be happening in Memphis. He said he had found an apartment near the waterfront where he could operate. He used a name that I had used before, John Willard, an alias. He told me to meet him there on the ground floor, which was a tavern, the next afternoon at three. Then he left taking the Remington, still in the box it had been wrapped in. It was still raining when he drove off.

"By morning it had stopped raining and I drove around and had lunch until it was time to meet with Raoul. I noticed my right tire had lost so much air it was almost flat, so I pulled over to the side of the road and fixed it. That took about twenty minutes. I then found a commercial parking lot on the perimeter of downtown Memphis and asked the attendant for directions to Main Street. On Main Street, I asked a policeman for directions to South Main. I found the place and went in and ordered a beer.

"I looked around for Raoul but didn't see him. I did notice two characters who appeared to be looking me over. I had been there several minutes when they left. I then asked the waitress if this was Jim's Grill. She informed me that Jim's Grill was just down the block. I got up from my unfinished beer and went down the street to the grill. It was three o'clock, the time for our meeting. I noticed the same two men sitting down and I couldn't escape the feeling that they were keeping me under some sort of surveillance.

"Since Raoul wasn't here I decided to get the Mustang and park it in front of the grill. No sense in paying when there was plenty of parking right in front of this place. I drove the Mustang back and parked in front, directly behind another car I vaguely recall was a pale yellow, too. When I went inside, Raoul was waiting for me, the other two characters gone.

"Raoul mentioned that the business with the gunrunners would take longer than anticipated and I should get a room upstairs. I agreed. I never learned whether or not Raoul had taken a room there. If he had signed the registration book, he hadn't used the name John Willard that I'd suggested the night before.

"In October 1974, in connection with the habeas corpus hearing to determine whether or not the State's accusation that I murdered Dr. Martin Luther King, Jr. should be put before a jury, my attorney subpoenaed this registration book in an attempt to discover who else had signed in. The Tennessee Attorney General's office responded that the book, a vital piece of evidence, had been lost.

"Raoul said he would be expecting visitors that evening and that I should be gone while he was taking care of business. He suggested I go to a movie and that he would be needing the Mustang that evening, and that I should go on foot.

"I remembered the flat spare tire and decided to have it fixed in case Raoul should have a blowout while conducting business. It must have been 5:45 when I eased the Mustang out onto Main Street heading north. I noticed a couple of service stations and pulled in asking if they could repair a tire. He commented that it was a busy time of day and that he'd try to get to it later. (The FBI in a letter to me asked for $1,700 to search the bureau's Martin Luther King, Jr. file for the information, which the bureau most likely has in its own classified records.)

"I then drove to another station and filled up. After leaving the area I drove in excess of two hundred miles without refueling. I pulled out of the area heading south, intending to circle around and repark the Mustang in front of the flophouse for Raoul's convenience. But when I pulled into South Main, I saw several uniformed police officers moving about in the general area of Jim's Grill. A police car was parked near the intersection. In addition, a policeman appeared to be blocking outgoing, while turning away incoming traffic. This development prevented me from turning right toward the rooming house, and forced me to turn left.

"Had the law latched on to Raoul with the guns? Instinctively, I switched on the radio and drove toward the southern edge of the city, intending to stop a safe distance away and telephone Raoul's intermediary in New Orleans. I would ask him to find out if a police raid had come down in or about the flophouse. As I neared the Tennessee-Mississippi line, I heard it on the news bulletin announcing the shooting of Martin Luther King, Jr. in Memphis. Minutes later, a follow-up newscast reported that police were looking for a suspect in the shooting: a white man in a white Mustang.

"I didn't need to hear any more bulletins to comprehend that it was best I move on to other pastures and dump the Mustang. About thirty minutes after the Rev. King was shot, an unidentified CB operator announced over channel 17 in Memphis that he was chasing at a high rate of speed a white Mustang he claimed was involved in the King shooting.

"It was proved to be a hoax. My prosecutors and the Memphis authorities would then actually defend the hoax by downplaying the extent to which it impeded law enforcement. They would say that the transmission had not been intended to distract police from the assassination area, despite the fact that several police cars were diverted from South Memphis by the broadcast. In their attempt to minimize the effect of the hoax, the authorities would claim that the hoaxer was a local teenager named Eddie Montedonico. Eddie, however, would disavow any participation in the incident.

"Was the North Memphis white Mustang hoax merely some crackpot's idea of a prank? I don't believe so. Consider its fruits: as a fiction created deliberately by a person or persons unknown, it is directly resulted in charging the Mustang with the potential for armed and dangerous flight to avoid prosecution. This would almost fatally prejudice anyone connected with a light-colored Mustang within several miles of the Rev. King's assassination at the time of the assault. Who other than Raoul and his network of associates had the capability of implementing such a hoax while also knowing the car I drove, my current residence, and my compromisable circumstances? I think no one, but the ultimate decision is the reader's.

"I drove all night and reached Atlanta. I parked the car and wiped all the fingerprints off. Then, getting a bus, I went back to Canada. My quest for liberty had brought me full circle. Here I was, back in Canada, still looking for bogus travel documents that would permit me to leave the confines of North America.

"Raoul and his people had left me with only about twelve hundred dollars, not enough to afford an extended voyage such as, for instance, to Australia. In my previous Canadian experience, I had been excessively cautious when investigating procedural requirements necessary in applying for a passport, inquiring of travel agencies by telephone rather than by personal appearance. This second time, with the lynch squads not far behind, my need for a travel document was on an 'or else' basis, dictating against an overabundance of caution.

"On April 19, fifteen days after the shooting of the Rev. Martin Luther King, Jr., the FBI announced publicly that they had identified Eric S. Galt as James Earl Ray, an escaped convict. According to the bureau, Memphis police had recovered both the rifle I had purchased in Birmingham and, lying on the sidewalk near the door, the overnight case I had taken into Bessie's flophouse.

"The report went on to state that the Rev. King had been shot while standing on the balcony of the Lorraine Motel, about three hundred feet from the rear entrance of the flophouse. Explaining how they identified me as being Eric Galt, the bureau claimed that when the discarded items were examined on April 5th in FBI headquarters, several fingerprints were found, including one on the rifle, and that fourteen days later the prints were identified as mine. The state would subsequently claim that due to the particular type of ammunition used in the shooting, Remington-Peters Soft Point, ballistics could not connect the murder slug with the rifle I had purchased. However, when CBS-TV apparently thought otherwise and petitioned Tennessee courts for an order to permit the network to conduct its own ballistic tests, the courts refused.

"On May 2, Kennedy Travel notified me that the Sneyd passport had been received from the authorities. I zipped over to their offices like Road Runner and collected the document along with a round trip to London on British Overseas Airways.

"I then exchanged the return portion of the ticket for passage to Lisbon, Portugal, and departed that evening in a Portuguese airliner. While at the Pax, I purchased a copy of *Life,* May 3, 1968, edition and saw a story entitled 'The Accused Killer; Ray Alias Galt, The Revealing Story of a Mean Kid.' That cover gave me a frightening glimpse of the savage legal lynching the American press was preparing for me.

"The *Life* article quickened my pace, and I decided to try Ian Colvin's contacts in Brussels. On June 8th, I caught a taxi to Heathrow Airport for the flight to Belgium. I presented my Sneyd passport to the control officer at the departure gate. He hesitated a moment, then politely asked me to step into an anteroom for a few questions. I agreed.

"In the small cell-like enclosure with a switchboard to one side, a second officer stood waiting. Instantly, they both latched onto me and commenced a search that produced the .38 pistol I'd bought in Alabama. They announced that I would be detained.

"From Wadsworth Prison I wrote two well-known American attorneys, F. Lee Bailey of Boston and Arthur J. Hanes, Sr. of Birmingham, inquiring if either would consider representing me when I returned to the United States in order to avoid having a Department of Justice bureaucrat say I confessed or made incriminating statements in respect to the King case before I could obtain counsel. I contacted Mr. Bailey and Mr. Hanes because they were the only two attorneys of prominence that I knew of.

"Mr. Bailey communicated negatively, mentioning something about a conflict of interest problem. In later years, Mr. Bailey would become a mouthpiece of sorts for the prosecution in the King case.

"Arthur Hanes, Sr. replied in the affirmative. But Mr. Eugene opposed the entry of Mr. Hanes into the case, saying that the United States Embassy had informed him that bringing Arthur Hanes into the Martin Luther King, Jr. matter would be unwise.

"Arthur Hanes made three trips to London. In the first, the British government refused his request to see me. In the second he received permission but we could discuss nothing of substance about the King case because two prison guards were stationed directly behind us, one on either side. The only legal thing we talked about was I gave Mr. Hanes power of attorney to sign literary contracts with author William Bradford Huie. Mr. Huie intended to write a series of articles about the case prior to trial.

"On July 19, Scotland Yard officers transported me from Wadsworth Prison to a United States Air Force base outside London, where a jet waited. The plane landed at Millington about 4 A.M. From the base a tank-like bus took us to the Shelby County jail in downtown Memphis.

"I was confined to a cellblock containing eight individual cells, all unoccupied except mine. There had obviously been a great deal of preparation, the entire cellblock having been refurbished solely on the occasion of my arrival. All the windows had been sealed shut with thick metal plates, the fresh air being replaced by a blower vent which blasted the cellblock with intermittently warm and cold air. Nor was there any sunlight, so essential to good health; both the cellblock and the individual cells were flooded with bright, artificial light from bulbs that burned twenty-four hours per day. The impossibility of telling day from night very quickly confused one's body calendar, disturbing organized thinking.

"Two television cameras were trained on the area twenty-four hours per day. One monitored my every movement in the cell; the other monitored activity in the surrounding cellblock. Two guards were stationed in the cellblock with me twenty-four hours per day. Finally, an open microphone capable of picking up the sound of a roach crawling across the floor had been installed in the cellblock. Although the sheriff's office gave its assurances that the microphone was turned off during critical consultations between my attorneys and myself, we have nothing more than the sheriff's word for it. In 1976, the United States Court of Appeals for the Sixth Circuit would conclude that my prison conversations had indeed been monitored but that such electronic surveillance was proper when the state managed to obtain a plea of guilty.

"A conflict developed between me and Mr. Hanes about the literary contracts with Mr. Huie. Another dispute arose over whether or not I should take the witness stand at trial. As Judge Battle would later confirm in the March 17, 1969, *New York Times,* I felt it essential to testify in my own defense, while Mr. Hanes disagreed. I didn't know that Mr. Huie had already prevailed upon Mr. Hanes through the no deal clause in their contracts to keep me off the witness stand. Now, why would Mr. Huie want me not to testify?

"Less than a week before the trial was to begin, word reached Mr. Huie of my determination to take the stand. He forthwith summoned Jerry from St. Louis to his base of operations, set him up in a motel and told him the finances of the King case. He said his publishers were footing the bills for the defense, and Hanes must perform according to Mr. Huie's instructions.

"In other words, my silence would enable Mr. Huie and his New York supports to publish their version not only of the King murder but also of my testimony relative thereto.

"I decided to get another attorney and found Mr. Foreman. Mr. Foreman spent about ten minutes looking through the files of my case before going out to dinner with Arthur Hanes. I would learn this many years later as Arthur Sr. would recall that, 'We tried to outline the case to him but he didn't seem too interested. We offered him everything we had, but he took nothing with him. He wasn't interested in the case. He wanted to drink and talk about his famous case.'

"Having seen the fruits of Percy Foreman's representation of me, Arthur Hanes Sr. would say in 1976, 'My judgment is that the man never even considered trying the case. Far as I can ascertain he never prepared and he never investigated. He never considered giving James Earl Ray a trial. For what reason I don't know.'

"Certainly the two most significant questions in the whole case were 'Was there a conspiracy to kill Dr. King?' and 'Did James Earl Ray fire the weapon?' Percy Foreman never asked me either question. This he would confirm at a Foreman press conference on March 11, 1969.

"It was not until February 3 that I saw my attorney again, on the occasion of his popping into jail with another contract for me to sign. While Mr. Foreman rattled persuasively on about how he fully expected acquittal from our jury trial, I went through the motions of reading and signing the contract. There was little will to resist left in me after nearly seven months of psychologically debilitating incarceration. The document provided that, in return for Percy Foreman's defense of me, 'in trial or trials' pending in Memphis, Tennessee, I would authorize all past and future funds accruing from literary contracts to be paid directly to Percy Foreman at his office in Houston, Texas.

"I signed a paper for Percy Foreman reflecting that he advised me to let him negotiate a guilty plea, but I informed him that I didn't intend to enter such a plea in the case.

"He said it was in my best interest to plead guilty because the news media, including *Life* and *Reader's Digest,* had already convicted me through prejudicial pretrial publicity. He said the court clerk could and would manipulate the pool of jurors in a manner that would result in all blacks and chamber of commerce types.

"Lastly, he revealed he had brought John Jay Hooker, Sr. into the case; his son was destined to become Tennessee's next governor, and with Mr. Foreman's intimate connections with the Hooker family, a pardon would be arranged after I had served two or three years in prison.

"As to the potency of Charley Stephens's testimony, I believe that Mr. Foreman knew, but did not tell me, that the prosecution for many reasons would never be so foolish as to have Charley subjected to cross-examination on the witness stand. I would discover many years later that Mr. Foreman had obtained a sworn affidavit from a Memphis cab driver named James H. McGraw that impeached Stephens's testimony. Mr. McGraw's affidavit reads in part:

"'On April 4, 1968, I was driving a Yellow Cab and was dispatched to 422½ So. Main St. to pick up a fare. When I arrived at this address, I observed two white Mustangs parked at the curb. Upstairs I found the fare to be Charles Stephens who was lying on the bed in a very drunken condition. Due to this condition I returned to the cab, made a U-turn and went south on Main Street. When I got to the corner of So. Main and Calhoun Streets, the dispatcher said that Dr. M. L. King had been shot.'

"But Percy Foreman knew the prosecution was afraid of an even greater threat than McGraw's testimony: the refusal of Grace Walden Stephens to corroborate her husband's testimony incriminating me. Mrs. Stephens could have been made rich overnight if she had only supported her husband's sworn statement. But her integrity could not be compromised by the state's offer of bribe money.

"Her principles cost Grace Stephens much much more than the loss of riches. The news media soft-pedaled the fact that on July 8th, she was taken by her husband and Memphis police officers to John Gaston Hospital for treatment of an ankle injury. However, during treatment, a psychiatrist suddenly appeared and, in an instant diagnosis, said her problem was mental. He had her committed to Gaston's psychiatric ward.

"Grace was forcibly confined for three weeks until she was taken before Judge Harry Pierotti, who ordered her committed to Western State Psychiatric Hospital, where she would remain until after the prosecution had obtained a guilty plea in the King case.

"Ten years later her release would be demanded by a group of ministers, including the Rev. James Lawson (at whose invitation Dr. King had come to Memphis and the Lorraine) and attorney/author Mark Lane.

"Mr. Foreman threatened that if I didn't plead guilty to the murder of Dr. Martin Luther King, Jr. government agents were likely to arrest my brother Jerry and charge him with conspiracy to murder Dr. King. Further, Mr. Foreman told me that my seventy-year-old father would be arrested and returned to an Iowa prison from which he had escaped some forty years previous.

"Finally, sometime around the later part of February, I tentatively agreed to enter a plea of guilty. Because of the design of my detention, I probably was not in the best physical or mental shape to engage in constructive, long-range thinking, or to effectively contest the forces maneuvering for the plea. In fact, on reflection, I suspect it was almost a feeling of relief to enter a plea, and thus perhaps escape the Darkness at Noon.

"Once he had my agreement in hand, Percy Foreman went back and forth to the attorney general's office with the stipulations for me to sign. The stipulations detailed a step-by-step account of what the prosecution would have presented as the state's version of the King homicide in a trial. Foreman would checkmark with a pencil the stipulations I objected to, then have me initial the page indicating I agreed to all but the checked stipulation on that particular page. The crafty Percy Foreman would later produce for use against me a set of the original stipulations, providing also a set for the attorney general's office. My signature of approval appeared on each page, but someone had erased the penciled check marks where I had objected to the stipulations.

"My brother John visited, and I mentioned to him that I would like to withdraw Foreman from my case and make an attempt to defend myself. These remarks promptly reached the news media and it caught the eye of Percy Foreman.

"The following day in Houston, Foreman phoned William Bradford Huie wondering if he still had me as a client. Foreman returned to Memphis and visited me in jail. He appeared somewhat overwrought and again implied that if he were forced to try the King case, he wouldn't put forth his best effort, and also mentioned the possibility of family members going to jail for one or more reasons if I forced the issue. It was during this meeting on March 9 that I actually agreed not to stand trial for the assassination of Dr. Martin Luther King, Jr.

"On March 11, 1969, I was taken to Nashville Prison where I was taken to the segregation. This building was called Unit 6. The interior of the place consisted of two small rooms in the front section situated on either side of a lobby. The lobby was furnished with a desk in which the keys were kept. The prisoners were kept in the rear section of the building, which was made up of four narrow walks or halls, thirteen cells to the walk, except for number four walk, which accommodated only eight cells. Here the electric chair took up the extra five-cell space.

The next day Ray was interviewed by a high-ranking prison official. "He said he thought I had been properly tried and convicted and said he knew I had buried loot, and offered to dig it up for me, and place it in a bank for my exclusive use if I would confide in him its location. He went on to say if I cooperated with him, and did not appeal my conviction, I would be treated like any other prisoner.

"Back in my cell, I wondered if this official had been serious or was suffering from a mental impairment sometimes associated with the aging process. I had never met a lawman who offered to dig up a prisoner's ill-got gains and deposit it in the bank for the personal use of the culprit. Nor have I heard of any such offer since then.

"I wrote a letter to the judge that Foreman was no longer representing me in any capacity. At this time my brother contacted attorney Richard J. Ryan of Memphis for assistance. He agreed to help us and came to Nashville to visit me in his status as defense attorney in the King case. Commissioner Harry Avery refused to admit Mr. Ryan into the prison. He said I would never be released from segregation so long as he was commissioner of corrections.

"Denied an attorney to help me demand a new trial, I wrote out in longhand a petition and mailed it to Judge Battle. The petition requested the court to grant me a hearing before the expiration of the thirty-day time limit governing the filing of a motion for new trial. For grounds, I cited Percy Foreman's conduct in misleading the court by reneging on his promise not to enter into literary contracts pending trial. I knew Judge Battle was aware that Foreman had violated the court's order; I thought that by formally raising the issue by motion, the judge would have to rule officially on the misrepresentation, rather than continue ignoring or finessing it. But Judge Battle would never render any further opinions in the case.

"The judge had been on vacation and didn't return to his official duties until March 31. Sometime that afternoon, while perusing the papers I had mailed him, he asked one of the assistant prosecutors, James Beasley, to contact the prison and find out who I intended to have represent me in my petition for a new trial. A prison official relayed the judge's inquiry to me and I gave him the name of Richard J. Ryan. Later that afternoon, when Mr. Beasley entered Judge Battle's office to give him Ryan's name, he found the judge slumped over my papers on his desk, dead of what would be described as a cardiac arrest.

"I believe that Judge Battle's action in contacting me about representation is an indication that he was seriously considering my petition. While his death obviously precluded him from setting aside the guilty plea and ordering a public trial, it caused a big headache amongst the no-trial crowd.

"Media speculation appeared to revive anxiety among the Tennessee legal establishment luminaries that there might be a jury trial after all in the King murder case. The state gave a rare display of how little the law means to those who must live by it but who also have power to decide it. The day after Judge Battle's passing, the Honorable Hamilton Burnett, Chief Justice of the Tennessee Supreme Court, informed the news media that I was not entitled to a trial under provisions of Tennessee Statute 17-117.

"Whether Judge Burnett's remarks to the news media were intended as a message to lower court judges not to order a public trial in the King case is conjectural. But the Tennessee court's own ethics code considers it inappropriate for a jurist publicly to express an opinion about a legal issue that he may be called upon to adjudicate, particularly when he hasn't even had an opportunity to review the legal briefs submitted by attorneys for the opposing parties.

"But Judge Burnett's extra judicial pronouncement reached its desired mark, for when Mr. Ryan (who, by the way, did finally receive certification with Mr. Hill to represent me) petitioned the Tennessee courts for a new trial under the very clear mandate of the 17-117 statute, all the lower court judges ruled against him. Interestingly, when the Tennessee Supreme Court ratified the lower court rulings, Justice Burnett—surely for ethical reasons—excused himself from the case.

"Near the town of Petros, forty miles west of Knoxville, Brushy Mountain is a secluded Tennessee penitentiary that achieved maximum security status in 1968. Except for the front extrance area, Brushy is surrounded by the Appalachian Mountains. The only way to Brushy is a winding gravel road that leads off Highway 116 approximately one mile away. I was sent there and after putting in a few days in segregation I was put in C-Block.

"I decided that I needed to escape and recruited a helper who lay hands on the equipment that I would need. By April 1971, everything was ready for the escape attempt. I didn't make it as the interior of the tunnel was excruciatingly hot. It drove me out of the tunnel and into pondering alternative routes of escape. But then, suddenly I was besieged by nearly a dozen guards, brandishing shotguns and side arms. I was held in segregation for two months.

"In May 1981, two months after I had submitted my answers to the Board of Parole's questions pertaining to the King case, a fight erupted in the prison recreation building between two gangs, one white, the other black.

"About a week later, I was in the law library, which had been described as being a death trap. A few months earlier Warden Davis had ordered the library and other areas of the building restructured. Before the restructuring prisoners could circulate throughout the three sections of the single story building by way of portals in the rear of each partitioned-off section. These portals also permitted guards to circulate through the entire building. The warden's restructuring included having iron grilles bolted over the portals and a wire fence put up between the law library and the regular library, leaving only one small entrance in and out of the law library.

"I sat down at the table, spread my papers out, and began studying. Minutes later, someone grabbed me from behind, pinning my arms. I saw it was a black prisoner, and immediately I saw a knife coming at me, wielded by another black prisoner. I moved about to avoid the knife as much as possible, while at the same time hollering for assistance in case someone I knew entered the building. The scuffle had been going on for what seemed to me about five minutes when the knife wielder, apparently tiring, threw down the weapon and fled the library with his cohort hot on his heels. Thinking they might return in any second, I crawled over and picked up the blade. It was about a foot long. Within a few seconds I heard approaching voices, and directly several guards entered the room, followed shortly by Warden Davis himself. I vividly recall how unsurprised the warden appeared to be at the spectacle of one of his charges hacked up with a shiv. Whether he expected the stabbing is only speculative; since he had entered the prison system in 1948, he could well have considered the incident rather routine. Anyway, within five minutes the stretcher bearers arrived and moved me to the prison infirmary. From there I was hauled by ambulance approximately fifteen miles to a hospital in the city of Oak Ridge, Tennessee. It took 77 stitches to close the wounds. I was chained to the bed so I wouldn't escape.

"I was moved at two o'clock in the morning and taken to the main prison in Nashville, Tennessee. After this my wife Anna moved from Knoxville to Nashville. She would then drive to Knoxville a couple times per week to deliver her paintings to galleries. I was able to see her only twice a week, for an hour each time.

"There is one last possibility for a trial of the Martin Luther King, Jr. murder in the United States. The basis for the trial is a glaring error Judge Preston Battle made in the most primitive stages of the King prosecution.

"It had been rumored in the 1970s that Judge Battle had appointed Shelby County public defender Hugh W. Stanton, Sr. to represent Charles Quitman Stephens, the state's star witness in the King case, prior to the judge's appointment of Mr. Stanton to represent me in the same case. If true, Battle had placed Stanton in violation of the American Bar Association's Code of Professional Responsibility, which proscribes lawyers from representing multiple clients with differing interests in the same litigation. If true, Battle had committed an irreversible error.

"Acting on rumors, in 1982, I wrote the Shelby County Criminal Court Clerk, J. A. Blackwell, inquiring about the matter. In response, Mr. Blackwell's office, by letter dated 29 November 1982, stated, 'There was never a hearing held in criminal court in reference to Charles Quitman Stephens.' Although I assumed this to be a truthful communication, I nevertheless contacted the circuit court clerk, Clint Crabtree, on the chance that the circuit court may have been involved in the matter. The inquiry paid off. 'Yes, documents showed there had been a legal proceeding in circuit court relating to the appointment,' wrote the clerk. The clerk's records indicated that the legal proceeding came about when segments of a criminal court

record had been transferred to the circuit court in a habeas corpus hearing
for Mr. Stephens in circuit court. And these records disclosed that Judge
Battle had indeed appointed Hugh Stanton, Sr. to defend Charles Stephens
as a material witness in the Martin Luther King, Jr. homicide before the
judge had appointed Mr. Stanton to defend me in the same case. Further,
the documents not only confirmed the appointment, but also established
that Judge Battle had ordered Mr. Stephens jailed as a material witness in
the case on the same day he appointed Stanton to represent Stephens. Some
representation!

"Fortunately for me, if the habeas corpus petition hadn't been filed in
circuit court, it's doubtful that I would have ever discovered the criminal
court proceedings, for obvious reasons. After obtaining the circuit documents, I sued in the Memphis federal court for access to the entire criminal
court record of the Stanton appointment to defend Stephens and cited as
defendants Judge Battle's successor, Judge William H. Williams, and criminal court clerk J. A. Blackwell. But the federal judge, Odell Horton, predict-
ably, in September 1983, summarily dismissed the lawsuit without even
requiring the defendants to answer the suit. I suspect his intent was to terminate the proceedings before I could purchase the documents, and with
the complete file immediately petition for a trial in the Martin Luther King,
Jr. case. But due to Judge Horton's ruling, the time-consuming appeals process was necessary. On appeal, the Sixth Circuit Court of Appeals, by order
issued in March 1985, did reverse Horton.

"The integrity of the defendants in the above case can be gauged by
their perjurious statements in the federal court after remand, statements
swearing that I had never requested a transcript of the Stanton appointment. This even though I had copies of their letters in response to my in-
quiries, saying there was no transcript. Of considerably more import is the
fact that the defendants concealed the record of Stanton's appointment for
three years, a delaying tactic that prevented me from filing the petition for
a trial of the King murder for three years. A tactic that would have ended
for all eternity the chance for a public trial in the King case if I had expired
during those three years in my nonviolent segregation confinement. The
case is still pending."

Support and Voices
for Reform

People Against the Death Penalty

We are all outraged by the actions of murderers. But in our attempts to punish the murderer, very little concern is actually shown for the victim's family. Killing the killer may satisfy our thirst for blood, but it does nothing to help those who have been harmed. We must find ways to direct some of the energy generated by our outrage into programs that will provide ongoing support to those who have been victimized.

> After news of a murder leaves the headlines, we rarely hear anything about the victim's family. We are left to imagine the anguish of their experience. . . .
>
> We assume, for instance, that friends and relatives rally around to support the victim's families. Often, however, those closest to them are so confused by their grief that they pull away, leaving them isolated. We assume that courts and the police keep the victim's family informed and help them through the early stages of anger, fear, and mourning. But they often have no contact with either the investigating officers or the district attorney prosecuting the case. Some families are even treated as if they were the criminals. — Doug Magee, *What Murder Leaves Behind: The Victim's Family*, Dodd Mead, 1983.
>
> The families of murder victims are often given little support from the community, which seems interested only in what they can contribute to the prosecution of the case. Their pain is exploited for the sake of sensational news stories and to further political careers. Worse, families often have to deal with intimations that the murder victim was partly to blame for his own death. The need for vengeance creates new victims. — Marie Deans, daughter-in-law of murder victim.

The list of victims does not stop with the family and friends. Research is showing us that many governors who have allowed executions have agonized over and deeply regretted their decisions, and that judges and jurors have paid dearly for the sentences they have handed down. Few proponents of the death penalty have witnessed the devastating effects that carrying out the sentence has on prison guards and administrators. Some have refused to carry out executions; others have left their jobs. There are other victims, but perhaps the saddest are our children who will have to shoulder the burder of this inhumanity all their lives.

The death penalty makes killers of us all. Some victims' families agree that the death penalty is wrong. Such responses often infuriate people, for it is difficult to justify an execution if those most directly affected by the crime oppose it. Thus families who dare to do so risk being ostracized.

After they sought clemency for the man who murdered their child, one Washington state couple were deluged by so much hate mail and so many telephone threats that they were forced to move to another state. And yet, the families of murder victims continue to oppose the death penalty.

"Capital punishment is not going to do anything for victims . . . if there's anything I've learned from my daughter's murder, that's it," says Doris Mote, mother of a 14-year-old rape and murder victim.

"If my father taught me anything about life, it is that God gives life and only He has the right to take it away. The God I came to know, through my father, was one of life and mercy and living, another chance to do better, not one of vengeance."—William Riley, Orlando, Florida. From a letter to Governor Bob Graham asking clemency for his father's murderer, James Dupree Henry. Henry was executed by the State of Florida on September 20, 1984.

"Killing convicted criminals is a simple way to deal with crime, but nurturing a civilization is not simple, regardless of how criminals are treated." —Tennala A. Gross, Greenville, North Carolina, sister of a murder victim.

"I believe the person or persons who kill by capital punishment are as guilty as the person who is being punished."—Virginia Foster of Knoxville, Tennessee, 1976.

Opposing the death penalty does not mean disregarding the families of victims who are too often forgotten and who need to be recognized as victims themselves.

What Victims Need

- They need to be kept informed of what is going on at various stages of the criminal proceedings.
- They need the assurance that their community cares about them and the tragedy that has befallen them.
- They need counseling programs and self-help groups specifically designed to help them work through their grief so that healing can begin.
- They need financial aid (funeral/medical expenses) especially when the victim has been the family breadwinner.

- They need the sensitivity of friends, the support of their churches and communities.
- They do not need to be treated as curiosities by the media, the public, even by acquaintances.
- They do not need yet another killing, this time one that is carried out in their names.

People Against the Death Penalty
P.O. Box 81
Fayetteville, New York 13066

Southern Prisoners'
Defense Committee

The Southern Prisoners' Defense Committee was started in 1976. It was originally started to improve prison and jail conditions. When the program first got started, however, it was repeatedly asked to intervene in capital cases. A lot of people were left on death row without counsel and so, being one of the few legal organizations in this part of the country (and the group's states include most of the death belt states where the death penalty is given most frequently and the resources are the fewest) the committee was constantly called upon to respond in an emergency situation with people who were facing the death penalty. For the last 14 years the organization has been involved in this work.

The Southern Prisoners' Defense Committee provides free legal assistance to prisoners from Virginia to Texas, down through the Southeast. It has sought to enforce the Constitutional prohibition on cruel and unusual punishment in jails and prisons of the South. It has raised various human rights issues regarding who should be in prison and for how long, whether certain forms of punishment are excessive, and what standards govern how prisoners are housed, fed, and treated. It has pressed for alternatives to incarceration.

The South imprisons a greater percentage of its population than any other region of the country, and the higher incarceration rate is not attributable to a higher crime rate. Persons are sent to prison for substantial periods for minor offenses ranging from writing bad checks to traffic offenses. The mentally ill are often warehoused in jails or prisons after committing petty crimes.

In Alabama, a pregnant woman was sentenced to five years in prison for writing a bad check for $300. A 74-year-old man served a year in prison for driving without a license. The length of actual time served in the South is almost 50 percent longer than in the rest of the country.

More black people are in prison in the South than in any other region of the country. The South sentenced more people to death than any other region.

For more than a decade, lawyers with the Southern Prisoners' Defense

Committee have represented prisoners in challenges to cruel conditions and excessive and inhumane forms of punishment.

The committee has counseled prisoners and their families, investigated correctional systems, obtained court orders prohibiting certain practices and setting standards for humane operations, vigilantly monitored the enforcement of those decrees, and helped establish support groups for incarcerated people.

The committee has also punished legal assistance to those facing the most severe punishment of all — the death penalty. The committee's lawyers have represented death sentenced persons directly and provided materials and assistance to other attorneys representing those facing capital punishment.

The committee was created by the Southern Coalition on Jails and Prisons, a grassroots prisoners support organization, in response to the need for a regionally based program that provides prisoners with legal assistance. It was modeled after the Mississippi Prisoners Defense Committee, which has successfully challenged conditions at Mississippi's only penitentiary. David Lippman, an attorney, was one of the founders of the Southern Prisoners' Defense Committee and continues to serve on the board of directors.

The Defense Committee's efforts on behalf of prisoners have brought about more decent and humane prison conditions, limits on the number of prisoners for certain facilities, creation or improvement of rehabilitation, vocational and educational programs, improved medical care, better training for guards, fairer treatment for prisoners and other reforms.

The committee's litigation has forced legislatures and executives to come to grips with the costs and dangers of sending so many people to prison for so long. It has required them to consider and implement alternatives to incarceration.

The committee's capital punishment litigation has resulted in a number of death sentences being set aside and important precedents being established. The committee also raises the issues of race and poverty in the imposition of the death penalty, in the courts and in public forums as well. And the committee serves as a resource center for lawyers involved in any stage of capital litigation.

The Defense Committee has responded to an urgent need for legal assistance to those facing execution. There are only a handful of lawyers and programs that specialize in the defense of capital cases. "All that stands between the men, women and children on death row and execution are two dozen dedicated attorneys," wrote one reporter.

Most of the Southern states have no public defender programs and provide only the most minimal compensation for attorneys who take death cases. The result is, at best, lawyers who do not specialize in capital punishment law and at worst, lawyers who care nothing about the person they are defending.

Tom Wicker, of the *New York Times*, has observed that "something near a pattern of inadequate or incompetent legal representation can be found in death penalty cases, particularly in the South, particularly for poor and uneducated persons."

The state is obligated to provide a poor person accused of a capital crime a court-appointed lawyer only at trial and one appeal to the state supreme court. After that, a condemned person is on his own to obtain representation in order to seek review by the United States Supreme Court or the lower federal courts. Many do not find assistance until execution is imminent.

The Defense Committee has repeatedly come to the rescue of inmates who are as close as a week to execution but without counsel. The Defense Committee has won new trials or sentencing hearings by showing fundamental violations of the Constitution.

Stephen Bright, Director
Southern Prisoners' Defense Committee
185 Walton Street, N.W.
Atlanta, Georgia 30303

Reconciliation Ministries

Reconciliation Ministries is a private not-for-profit organization founded in Nashville, Tennessee, to help prisoners' families and in so doing help prisoners themselves. When prison threatens to tear families apart and separate people from their friends, Reconciliation tries to help lessen the burden and keep families together.

Jeff Blum and Kaki Friskics-Warren founded the organization in 1984. They started out working with the men on death row, counseling them and getting personal things for them such as cards and stamps and other things they needed. With a change in administration, they were no longer allowed to go back on the row to visit with the men, so they decided to work with the families and Reconciliation House was born.

The group Separate Prisons was started in October of 1985 by Zel Morris, Shirley Vanarsdale, Cheryal Smith and Friskics-Warren. This was a support group of women who each had a loved one in prison. They talk to each other, voice their fears and hopes, and offer comfort to each other in times of trials and heartbreak. They support each other like a big family. They are not shunned by each other as they sometimes are by outsiders who find out they have someone in prison. These women are victims of society just by loving someone in prison.

One way to ease the fear and stress prison causes is to inform families about prison and prison-related issues. Reconciliation's caring staff learns what prisoners' families need through support group meetings, phone calls, cards, letters, and personal visits. What goes on during these one-on-one exchanges is personal and confidential. However, with concerns that are common to many families, Reconciliation members can unite their many voices into one strong voice that the prison system and the community at large will hear.

Only when people hear what is going on can they respond, and they do. Reconciliation is supported entirely by donations from individuals, churches and businesses who believe in justice, mercy, and reconciliation. The group receives no state or federal money.

Reconciliation offers many services to families of prisoners in Tennessee, including the Reconciliation House in Nashville, which welcomes visitors from out of town who come to visit a Nashville prison. The Guest

House provides beds, towels, linens, a stocked kitchen for guests to use, a living room with a wide-screen TV, and a playroom full of toys for children. There's always a family feeling at the Guest House both from the staff and the guests.

Maps and prison information are available, and if you need help with transportation notify Reconciliation when you make your reservations at least a week in advance. The Guest House is free of charge, but donations are always accepted.

Separate Prisons Support Group

In a society that often shuns the families and friends of prisoners, many parents, spouses, and children find themselves driven into a sort of hiding. They often live isolated and ostracized lives. Their prison is not constructed of walls and bars. Instead, they are in separate prisons, held by fear, prejudice, and loneliness.

Separate Prisons is a support group for women who have loved ones in prison. At Separate Prisons, these women can meet and talk with other women in similar situations. They can voice their fears, express their hopes, and offer ways of coping with frustration.

They support each other with empathy that can be found nowhere else. Group activities may include listening to a speaker invited to inform the group about a prison-related subject, or discussing a topic picked by the group at a previous meeting. If a group member has a pressing issue, the group helps her through it. Not only do the members talk, but they take action, too.

Each year there is a Youth Wilderness Camp that is organized for youths between 12 and 16 years of age with an incarcerated parent. They will participate in camping, hiking and other outdoor activities. More importantly, they will explore their feelings and values with trained adult leadership and return to their community more confident and responsible for their own behavior.

Nashville Separate Prisons Group
P.O. Box 90827
Nashville, Tennessee 37209
(615) 292-6371

Death Penalty Resistance Project

The Death Penalty Resistance Project believes that it is the duty of the state of Tennessee to protect the lives of all persons within its jurisdiction, including both victims and perpetrators of violent crime. The Death Penalty Resistance Project believes that the death penalty is the ultimate cruel, inhumane, and degrading punishment and that the death penalty violates all human rights by violating the right to life while failing to compensate the victims of violent crime.

The Death Penalty Resistance Project has local chapters in the major cities of Tennessee, a steering committee, and members from across the state. The members of the Death Penalty Resistance Project are working to achieve an ultimate goal: the abolition of capital punishment in Tennessee.

The Death Penalty Resistance Project is involved in a major restructuring aimed at forming a viable constituency capable of lobbying in the Tennessee legislature. Two major components of DPRP are to monitor death penalty–related activities including capital trials, public policy initiative, and other resistance activities, and to advocate alternatives to capital punishment through information dissemination and public witness.

The Death Penalty Resistance Project exists on the effort of volunteers and is therefore always in need of support . . . your support.

Members of the Death Penalty Resistance Project are kept abreast of activities at both the state and local levels through *Tennessee's Lifelines,* a publication of DPRP, and intermittent mailings concerning executions or pending legislation pertinent to the death penalty issue.

Members of the Death Penalty Resistance Project choose to involve themselves in a variety of ways: fund-raising activities, letter-writing campaigns, lobbying local legislatures, public speaking engagement or by simply supporting the project's efforts through financial donations.

Currently, the Death Penalty Resistance Project is funded solely by monetary donations of those who believe in the abolishment of capital punishment. The group invites you to join in this important work through the contribution of time, money, or advice.

The death penalty, because it involves the deliberate taking of a human life, has always been an important issue for the people of Tennessee. The question of the morality of capital punishment as well as its effectiveness as a deterrent to violent crime has spurred a debate which continues to the present day.

Since becoming a state in 1796, Tennessee has legally executed 305 people. In 1913, Tennessee made the change from hanging to electrocution for the sake of decency and humanity, and an electric chair was installed at the state prison.

The Tennessee electric chair has claimed 125 lives — men who were executed for crimes of rape, assault with intent to rape, and murder. Of those electrocuted, 85 were black, 40 were white. Maurice Mays, a black man electrocuted in 1922, was exonerated five years after his death when a white woman confessed to the crime. The most recent execution occurred in 1960 when William Tines was killed for the crime of rape.

Since 1960, executions have been delayed by legal battles over the constitutionality of capital punishment. In 1976, however, the U.S. Supreme Court cleared the way for execution of people convicted of first-degree murder. Tennessee's death row has been growing rapidly over the years. As legal appeals are exhausted we draw closer to the time when we will, once again, strap a human being into a chair and kill him.

The death penalty can be based upon the assumption that we as Americans have an infallible judicial system. However, the death penalty relies on human nature and thus will always be a system that issues a death sentence to a racial, social, or economic minority.

Death Penalty Resistance Project
P.O. Box 120552
Nashville, Tennessee 37212

Tennessee's Death Row

This chapter is offered in the hope of giving readers some added insights into the issue of capital punishment and its victims in the state of Tennessee. It is also hoped that this offering will generate some support among those who oppose the electrocution of human beings as a form of punishment in this state.

Innocent people are executed. It is often hard to know or find out about because once someone is dead, no one is going to spend time or money investigating the crime again, since it's too late to correct if a person is innocent. But cases have been discovered in which innocent people were executed.

Maurice Mays was executed in Tennessee in 1922 for killing a white woman. Six years later, another white woman confessed to the murder, telling how she had dressed up as a man and had blackened her face and hands before killing the woman for having an affair with her husband. She did this, of course, to throw the blame on a black man. And it worked because when she did confess, six years after Mays had been electrocuted, authorities told her they weren't interested because they had already punished someone for that murder.

Harry W. Forgl, Chief Judge for the Sixth Judicial Circuit, Florida, stated that he knew of four persons from his own experience who were sentenced to die and were later proven innocent.

A careful study of the death penalty between 1972 and 1980 showed that black killers and killers of whites were substantially more likely to receive a death sentence. In Florida, for example, a black offender convicted of killing a white was 40 times more likely to be sentenced to death than someone (white or black) who killed a black. In Georgia, a convicted murderer was 10 times as likely to get a death sentence when the victim was white. In that state from 1976 to 1980, 35 whites killed blacks but only one was sentenced to death; although 310 blacks killed other blacks, only 11 were sentenced to death.

The odds of receiving a death sentence when the victim is white are about 12 times greater in Tennessee than in a comparable case in which the victim is black. In most Tennessee counties, no whites have ever been prosecuted for the death penalty when the victim was black. But blacks make up nearly half of the homicide victims in the state each year.

The conclusion is obvious: in the trial courts of this nation, the killing of a white is treated much more severely than the killing of a black. Where the death penalty is involved, our criminal justice system functions as though white lives were more valuable than black lives.

Besides being racist, the death penalty is also classist in being applied. Both sex and socio-economic class are factors that help determine who receives a death sentence and who is executed. During the 1980s, only about 1 percent of all those on death row were women, even though women commit about 14 percent of all murders. Since 1930, only 33 women have been executed in the United States (14 of them black).

Often the poor in our society get executed. Poor people cannot afford to hire their own attorneys, so they have court-appointed lawyers who don't get very much pay to defend their clients and they don't have money to hire investigators or expert witnesses. More often than not, these attorneys have large case loads of clients, some paying, some not. So they sometimes don't devote a lot of time to the nonpaying, poor clients. Moreover, many of these court-appointed lawyers have little or no experience in murder trials and must face prosecutors who have years of experience. Thus the poor are the people who end up getting the death sentence. Rich people hire cracker-jack lawyers and pay them a lot of money, and they get off with a lesser sentence—if they are convicted at all—for the same crimes. Capital punishment means that those without the capital get the punishment.

Michael DiSalle, former governor of Ohio, said that during his experience he found that men on death row had one thing in common; they were all penniless. The fact that they had no money was a principal factor in their being condemned to death. Justice William Douglas noted in the *Furman* decision: "One searches our chronicles in vain for the execution of the affluent strata of this society."

Capital punishment is cruel and unusual. It is a relic of the old days of penology when slavery, branding, and other corporal punishments were commonplace. Like those other barbaric practices, it has no place in a civilized society.

The method of execution in the state of Tennessee is electrocution. The condemned prisoner is led, or most often dragged, into the death chamber and strapped into the electric chair. Electrodes are fastened to his head, arms, and legs. When the switch is thrown, the body strains, jolting as the voltage is raised to 2,500 volts, then lowered to 1,000, then raised and lowered again. Often smoke rises from the head and there is the awful smell of burning flesh. No one knows just how long electrocuted individuals retain consciousness.

In 1983, the electrocution of a prisoner in Alabama took over ten minutes and three jolts of electricity. A witness observed: "When he was hit with the first jolt, his body tensed and the strap on his left leg burst off. When the second jolt hit his body, he did not move, but a pool of smoke and a burst of flames came from his left temple, and more smoke came from his left calf. But the doctors said he was still not dead, so a third jolt was administered." The observer called it a barbaric ritual.

Because capital punishment is an emotional issue, many people don't stop to realize, or just don't know, that very few of those convicted of murder ever receive the sentence of death. And contrary to what many assume, it is rarely the worst of the worst who find themselves on death row. In the United States each year there are more than 20,000 murders committed, and approximately 450 are committed in Tennessee each year. So in the 11 years since the death penalty was reinstated in the U.S., more than 220,000 persons have been the victims of murder. Yet, there are only about 2,200 men and women on death rows in this country.

When the issues of violence and the increasing murder rate are discussed, the focus is almost always passed to the death penalty and death row. This wrongly gives listeners the impression that most, if not all, persons convicted of murder are subjected to the death penalty. And so, with an emotional fervor, many vote "yes" to executing murderers to rid society of this violence. The fact is that more than 98 percent of those convicted of murder don't receive a sentence of death, don't spend from eight to 14 years on death row waiting to be executed, but do, in some cases, have a chance of someday rehabilitating themselves and returning to society. So society's anger and desire for revenge is taken out on the few scapegoats unfortunate enough to have been selected for prosecution for the death penalty.

The Fourteenth Amendment to the United States Constitution supposedly guarantees each of us the right to due process of law, and equal protection of the laws. In part it states "that no State shall make or enforce any law which shall abridge the privileges or immunities of citizens of the United States; nor shall any State deprive any person of life, liberty, or property, without due process of law; nor deny to any person within its jurisdiction, the equal protection of the laws." When only a tiny percentage of all convicted murderers receive a sentence of death, there is no way this number could have been afforded due process or equal protection of the laws. The whole process of determining who winds up on death row is totally arbitrary and more like a lottery than any form of justice. Should the state adopt standard sentencing laws, which would make punishment for murder the exact same in all cases, we would have some fairness and proportionality in sentencing procedures.

In both rape and murder cases (since 1930, 99 percent of all executions have been for these crimes) there has been substantial evidence to show that courts have been arbitrary, racially biased, and unfair in the way in which they have sentenced some persons to prison but others to death. Racial discrimination was one of the grounds on which the Supreme Court relied in *Furman vs. Georgia* to rule the death penalty unconstitutional in 1972.

Statistics confirm this discrimination in applying the death penalty. Between 1930 and 1980, a total of 3,862 persons were executed in the United States. Of those, 2,066, or 54 percent, were black. For rape, 455 men were executed during this period, all but two in the South; 405, or 90 percent, were black. During these years, blacks made up about 10 percent of the country's population. The nation's death rows have always had a disproportionately large number of blacks relative to their fraction of the total population. In recent years, many have believed that such flagrant discrimination was a thing of the past, but since the death penalty was reinstated in 1977, about half of those on death row at any given time have been black. This is still a disproportionately large percentage given the black/white ratio of the total population.

But if discrimination is apparent in determining who is sentenced to death, then it has to be alarming when the race of the victims in these murders is considered.

Can you continue to consider the death penalty as something abstract because it is carried out behind the cold gray walls and bars of a prison, hidden away from society? Or should you consider its reality, and the fact that you sanction this barbaric taking of human life by remaining silent and not opposing legalized murder? There is no better example of premeditated, willful, and intentional murder than when the state confines a person to a small cell for some eight to fourteen years before finally carrying out the promise of taking his life that was made the day the prisoner entered death row.

We ask you to seriously consider the things that we have discussed here and voice your opposition to the death penalty. Life in prison may not seem like a lot to look forward to (and indeed it is not) but even under these conditions most would choose a life of confinement over a brutal death.

Write to the governor of Tennessee, State Capitol Building, Nashville, Tennessee 37219 and express your opinion.

Write letters to both your state senator and your congressmen expressing your opposition.

National Coalition to Abolish the Death Penalty
1419 V. Street NW
Washington, D.C. 20009

Amnesty International
by David Hinkley, Regional Director

Amnesty started in 1961 in London. It was started by a British lawyer and the focus of the organization has always been in three areas of human rights work. For prisoners, we work for the release of what we call prisoners of conscience, which is they don't believe in violence. The second area of our mandate is to work with all political prisoners, and third is to work for the abolition of all forms of torture, cruel and inhumane and degrading treatment, including executions which we regard as the ultimate form of cruel and inhumane treatment and a violation of life.

We've always been opposed to the death penalty but the work began to become much higher priority in 1977 when there was an international gathering in Stockholm which produced the Stockholm Declaration plan to fight the death penalty worldwide in a campaign style rather than just writing letters in behalf of individuals faced with execution. We would also confront legislation that kept the death penalty off the books and also do our best to create a public contingency against the death penalty.

In 1977 we began the extensive research and action on the death penalty, and it has remained one of the organization's top priorities ever since then. In the past twelve years, we have particularly focused on those countries which use the death penalty most often. About a hundred countries still have the death penalty on the books; some of them don't actually carry it out. In the '80s for example, six or eight countries were responsible for over 80 percent of all the executions in the world. Unfortunately the United States is one of those countries, along with the Soviet Union, Nigeria, South Africa, China, Iraq, and I believe Pakistan.

We also work for repeal of the death penalty in legislation. We have an international network. There are Amnesty International members in 160 countries. We have grown very dramatically over the years, numbering over 700,000 members. We don't get involved in prisoners of conscience or political prisoners in the United States. That's to protect our impartiality. We do work in our own country on the death penalty, which is vital for Amnesty USA because we don't want to be in the position of throwing stones on glass houses and from our own glass house. So we work extensively in the United States for abolition of the death penalty. As the large number of prisoners reach the end of their appeals we have begun to execute in large numbers in the past several years.

The right to life and the right not to be subjected to cruel, inhumane or degrading treatment of punishment are enshrined in the Universal Declaration of Human Rights and other international human rights documents. The death penalty is a denial of those rights and its use in the United States has resulted in violations of human rights throughout that country. Amnesty International is calling on the United States to join the growing number of nations all over the world who have abolished the death penalty or are working towards abolition. In its report on the death penalty in the United States, the organization included the following recommendations:

"All governments in death penalty states should abolish the penalty for all offenses in law.

"The death penalty should be abolished under the federal Uniform Code of Military Justice and the federal government should refrain from enacting the death penalty under federal civilian law.

"Pending the abolition of the death penalty in law, state laws and practice should conform to minimum international standards that preclude the imposition of the death penalty on juveniles or the mentally ill.

"Until the death penalty is abolished or a moratorium on death sentences is introduced, state governors and boards of pardons and paroles should broaden their criteria for granting clemency in capital cases.

"Amnesty International believes that the evidence of racial discrimination in the application of the death penalty is a matter of urgent concern and recommends that the executive or legislative branch of the federal government commission a thorough, impartial inquiry into the question."

Countless men and women have been executed for the stated purpose of preventing crime, especially the crime of murder. Yet as documented, study after study in diverse countries has failed to find convincing evidence that the death penalty has any unique capacity to deter others from committing particular crimes. The most recent survey of research findings on the relation between the death penalty and homicide rates, conducted for the UN in 1988, concluded that "this research has failed to provide scientific proof that executions have a greater deterrent effect than life imprisonment. Such proof is unlikely to be forthcoming."

Undeniably the death penalty, by permanently "incapacitating" a prisoner, prevents that person from repeating the crime. But there is no way to be sure that the prisoner would indeed have repeated his crime if allowed to live, nor is there any need to violate the prisoner's right to life for the purpose of incapacitation; dangerous offenders can be kept safely away from the public without resorting to execution, as shown by the experiences of many abolitionist countries.

If today's penal systems do not sanction the burning of an arsonist's home, the rape of a rapist or the torture of a torturer, it is not because they tolerate the crimes. Instead it is because societies understand that they must be built on a different set of values from those they condemn.

An execution cannot be used to condemn killing — it *is* killing. Such an act by the state is the mirror image of the criminal's willingness to use physical violence against a victim.

Related to the argument that some people deserve to die is the proposition that the state is capable of determining exactly who they are. Whatever one's view of the retribution argument may be, the practice of the death penalty reveals that no criminal justice system is, or conceivably could be, capable of deciding fairly, consistently, and infallibly who should live and who should die.

It is the irrevocable nature of the death penalty, the fact that the prisoner is eliminated forever, that makes the penalty so tempting to some states as a tool of repression. Thousands have been put to death under one government only to be recognized as innocent victims when another set of authorities comes to power. Only abolition can ensure that such political abuse of the death penalty will never occur.

There is no convincing argument that society cannot find ways other than killing to express its condemnation of crime. As has been found in countries where the death penalty has been abolished, a sufficiently severe punishment which is compatible with international human rights standards can adequately demonstrate society's condemnation of the crime in question. Unlike the death penalty, nonlethal punishments can reflect the values of society rather than the values of the killer.

I became involved in Amnesty in 1973. I was a volunteer for nine years and I've been on staff for seven years. I was involved in the death penalty issue long before I was with Amnesty. Since I've been on staff here in California, I've been working to develop state abolition teams all over the western United States. It's taken seven years but we now have state teams in all thirteen western states. For the country, we have teams in almost every state whether they have the death penalty or not making sure the state doesn't reintroduce the death penalty, making sure the public is informed of our position on it.

In the west our main interest is in California where we have over 250 people on death row. Nationwide the interest is in the south, where most of the people are being executed.

We do most of our work through letter writing, and we sometimes demonstrate and conduct vigils. We try to network with other abolitionist groups and build their activism up on the death penalty by providing them with our information and research and with organizational cooperation on projects like these in Sacramento.

Mothers Opposed to Maltreatment of Service Members

MOMS — Mothers Opposed to Maltreatment of Service members — was started in 1984 by Dorothy Warnacutt of Tennessee. She labored long hours, using household monies to alert Congress to the abuses of the Uniform Code of Military Justice. Broken in spirit when her cries went unheeded, Warnacutt became too ill to carry on and MOMS went dormant in early 1986.

Carolyn Dock, with the help of another Maryland couple and four former MOMS members, reactivated MOMS in May of 1987. The abuses of the UCMJ had to cease, and a support organization was badly needed.

Today the organization provides a worldwide network with regional representatives to act as an informational source and a support system for service members and their families. MOMS includes a cross section of concerned citizens, retired and active duty service members, and family and friends of incarcerated service members.

MOMS has a multiplicity of free services. It operates through donations and a $20 per year membership fee for those families that can afford it.

MOMS offers the following services:

1. *Legal.* Referral list of lawyers who are experienced in courts—martial, appeals, and upgrades of punitive discharges — with more than 100 law firms that accept cases and reduce their fees to MOMS members. They do charge a fee, however.

2. *Support.* Representatives in almost every state, Puerto Rico, and West Germany. Soon representatives will be in all areas where American service members are stationed. The representatives help the family understand the military system. They give emotional support and understanding, guide families through the agency maze, and help the families understand what to expect.

For the incarcerated service member, MOMS sends birthday and Christmas cards and a monthly newsletter to those who request it at the Disciplinary Barracks, the Marine and Naval brigs, and Army and Air Force stockades. The newsletter is a way of showing concern. Appropriate actions

158

are taken by MOMS to alert officials when problems surface at the correctional facilities.

3. *Parole.* Advice on preparing parole packets and information on how the system works.

4. *Ex-inmate/veteran benefits.* MOMS is doing a state-by-state and federal study to itemize those educational, training and medical benefits for which the former inmate can be eligible. We are networking with other support organizations who are concerned with halfway houses, job counseling and other state programs.

5. *Active Duty Areas.* Although this was not an area MOMS planned to be involved with, nonetheless it is. The organization has been involved with dependent problems referring the service member to appropriate agencies, lawyers, or organizations. MOMS gives its business card to active duty members who request it. Our hope is they can put it in their wallet and never have to take it out—but if that phone call has to be made, help will be available.

MOMS is a nationwide nonprofit organization, composed of civilians and active and retired military personnel. Its primary purpose is to ensure equal Constitutional protection for volunteer Armed Forces service members who protect the United States Constitution for all Americans.

MOMS is actively lobbying for fair and impartial courts-martial; military courts adhering to constitutional law and not rendering decisions based on the premise "for the good of the service"; punitive discharges being factored into sentences; military sentencing comparable to civilian sentences for similar offenses; military parole boards comprised solely of civilians; parole becoming a possibility to the 80 percent denied yearly; and military inspector generals becoming impartial investigators as mandated by Congress.

The MOMS organization was formed to bring public attention to injustices being suffered by members of the Armed Forces. These injustices are a result of command influence abusing the articles of the Uniform Code of Military Justice, for the purpose of preserving the image of the military.

MOMS
8285 Black Haw Ct.
Frederick, Maryland 21701
(301) 662-7643

The Death Penalty as a
Human Rights Issue

by Michael Radelet

Polonius: My Lord, I will use them according to their desert.
Hamlet: Use every man after his desert and who shall 'scape whipping? Use
them after your own honor and dignity. The less they deserve, the more
merit is in your bounty.

— Hamlet, Act II, Scene I

During the last decade, the popular and political arguments supporting America's use of the death penalty have been undergoing gradual and significant changes. First, now that most formal religious organizations have endorsed statements in favor of abolition, no longer are the arguments that God is a retentionist widely heard. Second, since it is now clear that executions cost many times more than an alternative sentence of life without parole (Garey, 1985), responsible retentionists no longer claim that hiring the executioner will save more tax money than feeding and housing "death row maggots." Third, the argument that executions will deter future murderers is endorsed by virtually no contemporary criminologists, and retentionists are left to speculate that this lack of deterrent effect results from the infrequency of the death penalty's use. Fourth, those who once argued that the death penalty is necessary to prevent convicted murderers from killing again or walking the streets after a short confinement have been silenced by research showing the probability of repeat homicide is minuscule (Marquart, 1989) and by the widespread availability of long-term or life imprisonment without parole (Wright, 1990).

Fifth, death penalty retentionists have conceded the inevitability of executing the innocent, although they argue this risk is small and outweighed by the death penalty's "moral benefits and the usefulness of doing justice" (van den Haag, 1986:1665). And, finally, retentionists are also troubled by the clear findings that the race of the victim correlates with sentencing outcomes, other factors being equal, though they respond that this simply means those who murder blacks should be sentenced more harshly.

Consequently, by admission of retentionists and even the Supreme

Court, today's support for the death penalty is increasingly centered on one issue: retribution. Because of the immense suffering caused by murderers, we kill them because we despise them and want them to suffer in return. Imprisonment for lengthy terms or even life is simply insufficient to give these animals their just deserts.

These changes in the nature of death penalty debates should be welcomed by abolitionists. After all, most abolitionists would be opposed to capital punishment even if it were cheap or even if it showed modest deterrent effects. They are just as opposed to the death penalty for black offenders, juveniles, the mentally ill, and the obviously guilty as they are opposed to its use on other prisoners. The abolitionist position argues it is no more possible to say certain categories of offenders are more deserving of execution than it is to say that some are more deserving of prolonged physical torture. And, the focus of the argument on retribution is in no small part a consequence of abolitionists' having won the debates on the other issues that have heretofore distracted the discussion. Long before retentionists, abolitionists have been arguing that retribution was the guts of the issue.

In this chapter, I would like to explore one aspect of human rights issues involved in retributive justifications for the death penalty (c.f. Grahl-Madsen, 1987). I will discuss the families of death row inmates. My data are experiential. Over the last decade I have testified in thirty death penalty cases and worked in one way or another, sometimes as a paralegal, on a hundred others. To varying degrees, I knew each of the last twenty men executed in Florida and have inherited property, arranged funerals, sprinkled ashes, and passed the eve of execution with several. I have also spent a few thousand hours housing and working with their families, and in five cases was with the mother or closest relative while their loved one was being killed.

My argument is:

1. An inclusive view of the "human rights" affected by capital punishment includes both the rights of the prisoner and the rights of the family. Specifically, the human right of relevance for families is that innocent people have a right to be spared terrible and avoidable agonies.

2. Experiencing the pains of the condemnation and execution of a loved one is a terrible and avoidable agony. Imprisonment, too, hurts the family, but this pain is unavoidable, and can be legitimated by society's right to protection (i.e., deterrence and incapacitation).

3. Even if just desert may, for the sake of argument, legitimate the pains the death penalty imposes on the guilty defendant, it does not justify the pains imposed on the defendant's innocent family members.

In a 1978 paper, Gibbs reviewed the difficulties of precisely defining retribution, but concluded that its essential ingredient is that retribution justifies punishment "solely for the reason that those on whom it is inflicted deserve it" (1978:294). It's just that simple: they deserve it. If one argued that retribution might justify torturing murderers, retentionists conventionally respond with the idea of *lex talionis*, a response that is not compelling because of its selective use (e.g., *lex talionis* would justify executing all murderers or raping all rapists). Further, *lex talionis* might justify torturing mass murderers or heinous murderers, an idea that most retentionists would reject.

Parenthetically, I note that the same reasons that make most reject corporal punishment on amorphous human rights grounds could also be used to reject the death penalty. Along these lines, in 1989, a Delaware legislator introduced a bill authorizing flogging for certain offenders, pointing out that if we can kill prisoners, "then I don't know why beating them is any worse" (*San Antonio Express–News,* Jan. 29, 1989). I agree completely, as the retributive doctrine draws no lines and would justify both. If retribution permits the state to kill its citizens, there is no clear reason why the doctrine would not allow the state to slice off the prisoner's legs.

Let us now take a closer look at the incremental suffering imposed by the death penalty that retributivists argue is deserved. As do life term prisoners, death row inmates face loss of liberty and all sorts of related pains. Confinement is quantitatively more painful for condemned prisoners than it is for other prisoners, in that various states may restrict death row inmates to their cells, cut off access to prison jobs, phones, classes, gyms, religious services, libraries, outside gifts, etc. But there are qualitative differences as well (Bedau, 1980: 162–64). Those serving life imprisonment do not have to cope with the anticipation of a preordained death, the uncertainty of appeals, the agony of losing best friends to the executioner, and the legally imposed label of not being worth living (Johnson, 1981). Compared to these, the issue of whether the death is by injection, electricity, or burning at the stake is trivial. I believe that these pains, in themselves, should be considered human rights abuses, but that is not my point today.

In my work with death row inmates, I have often found that the above pains are secondary to the anguish they feel when seeing what their death sentences put their families through. We often get a glimpse of this through the last words of executed prisoners, when families are regularly acknowledged and comforted. The primary component of the incremental increase of suffering caused by the death penalty over long imprisonment, as perceived by the inmate, is its impact on his family.

Death row inmates have good reasons to suffer because of what their predicament does to their moms and dads and kids, as the suffering of these family members is real and immense (Radelet et al., 1983; Vandiver, 1989). While I do not underestimate the tremendous suffering experienced by families of homicide victims, I also recognize the suffering of the families of the condemned. Perhaps one ought not to compare the anguish of families of murder victims with that of the families of death row inmates. Pain is pain, anguish is anguish, and each person's suffering reaches to immeasurable proportions. But whereas one suffers from the unpredictable behavior of individuals, the other suffers from the premeditated arm of the state.

Several incidents come to mind that justify this assertion. On April 18, the governor of Florida signed a death warrant on Marjorie Adams's son, her only child. Two days later, her husband, the condemned man's father, dropped dead. A fortnight thereafter, Mrs. Adams was back at the funeral home, this time to bury her son. In January I had the duty to call Louise Bundy to tell her that her son was dead. Ted Bundy never saw the 700 celebrants outside Florida's execution chamber, but his parents did, and it added to their anguish. Two weeks later I had to call her again to tell her that postautopsy pictures of her son were about to appear in a supermarket tabloid. Kay Tafero, while in Washington to bury her husband with military honors at Arlington Cemetery, learned that a death warrant had been signed on her only son. The next week, while visiting him in prison with a glass wall between them, Mrs. Tafero fainted when the prison's lights went out, as the auxiliary generator was being tested for its anticipated use in fueling the electric chair. A couple of years ago, Willie Darden's fiancée broke into an hysterical screaming fit in my front yard as she left for what she thought was to be her last visit.

I remember driving six members of a Bartow family to their home a few hours after their loved one was executed; the next morning the inmate's teenaged daughter, Regina Thomas, was hospitalized for what was described as a mental breakdown. Even though we get bulk discounts at Gainesville funeral homes, begging donations from churches and concerned citizens has left our bucket under many a dry udder. I hope never to see a better example of powerlessness than that felt by a family member while a loved one is being executed.

In large part, the death penalty is worse than life imprisonment because it terminates the opportunity to experience social relations (Bedau, 1980:163). But social relations are a two-way street; if you die, my opportunity to interact with you is just as destroyed as your opportunity to interact with me. In this, capital punishment hurts those with close relationships with the inmate as much as it hurts the prisoner himself. And, while the inmate foresees this with support from attorneys and ever-present comrades in neighboring cells, the family anticipates it with overwhelming helplessness and powerlessness, often in ignorance of criminal process and always in isolation. Much more than life imprisonment, death creates an "ever widening circle of tragedy" (Turnbull, 1978:54), claiming its victims with shotgun inaccuracy.

It should be noted that the actual punishment of death cannot be experienced by the prisoner. He can dread it, but because death extinguishes consciousness it cannot be experienced. So, capital punishment loses its object at the moment of its infliction. The family, however, remains to feel and absorb the loss. John Spenkelink has now been dead for 10 years, but I saw his mother in May and can assure you that her suffering is not over.

Few would deny that to kill the innocent is to violate their fundamental right to life. But many would agree that even worse than being killed ourselves would be to stand by helplessly as a loved one was being killed. Death row families are often bonded by the same unconditional love that bonds other families. They are no different. Having your child killed after a decade of design is an experience that can be worse than death itself. As Camus wrote, "the relatives of the executed man thereby experience a misery that punishes them beyond the bonds of all justice" (1959:30).

Back to the death penalty's retributive goal. Earlier I suggested that we be guided by the definition of retribution constructed by Gibbs: we use the death penalty because its victims deserve it. Problems of executing the innocent aside (Bedau and Radelet, 1987), the primary increase in suffering caused by the death penalty over life imprisonment is its vicariousness: it affects innocent family members as much as the guilty prisoner. A death penalty promoted on the basis of just desert cannot be just when it destroys the innocent as much as it punishes the guilty.

What remains is to discuss how the retributive justifications and consequences of the death penalty, in its effects on the innocent, can be viewed as a human rights issue. The concept of "human rights" is not the concept of a moral absolute; it is a social construction. Consequently, how social groups differ in time and place in their definition of such rights (see Bedau, 1982) is a more useful topic for discussion than specification of what a human right is or is not. Various governmental and international bodies have made several attempts to specify basic human rights (Amnesty International, 1987:3, 221–26; 1989: 82–85, 241–58). No matter how defined, these rights have meaning only when governments recognize and protect them. Indeed, the question of human rights can be viewed inversely as the question of what rights governments retain for themselves or what rights the people give to their governments.

In the United States, we have given our government far broader rights to kill the sons and daughters of our fellow citizens than the government actually exercises. After all, if our current death penalty statutes were used to their limits, far more people would be condemned and executed than is presently the case. Framing the issue in terms of governmental rights, rather than in terms of the human rights of killers or their victims, exposes the heart of the question. The question becomes what kind of society do we want to be.

I advance this thesis because I believe it may be useful in our death penalty debates of the 1990s. I believe the argument that the death penalty violates basic human rights of the prisoner, though correct, is not convincing to the public. After all, the unconditional love that a mother has for her son is not likely to be widely shared if her son turns out to be a heinous murderer. Those of us who work with death row inmates do not have a very likeable clientele, and it is difficult to generate much sympathy for them. But parents ought to be able to recognize the anguish of another parent. When the death warrant was signed for Dennis Adams, it was signed for Marjorie Adams's son. Coretta Scott King perhaps has said it best. Her husband was assassinated and her mother-in-law was murdered. Precisely because she knows the horror experienced when an innocent family is deprived of a loved one, she does not want that horror to be experienced by any other innocent family. "I could not support execution of their killers because it would be a disservice to all that Martin and his mother had lived for and believed" (King, 1986). What kind of society do we want to be?

Dr. Michael Radelet is a professor of sociology at the University of Florida in Gainesville. In addition to his well-known scholastic achievements, he provides housing for death row prisoners' families and occasional wayward abolitionists.